WHAT IF?

15 Topics Worth Discussing for Lifelong Happiness

Kurt & Katy Adkins

Some of the names in the testimonies that we have shared in this book have been changed to protect the privacy of the individuals involved.

WHAT IF?
15 Topics Worth Discussing for Lifelong Happiness
Kurt and Katy Adkins

Copyright© 2019 by Kurt and Katy Adkins
Published by Triple Threat LLC, Kalispell MT 59901
forfreedom5@yahoo.com
www.expandingtheeyeotthestorm.com

Cover design Katy Adkins

Edited by Donald Weise

ISBN: 978-1-7343873-1-5

To our dear friends Ron and Marthie Yeager,
Without your demonstration of unconditional love,
our hearts would have never opened to the idea
that God is Good!

Words can never describe how special you are to
both of us!

Thank you

FOREWORD

In our travels, Mary-Anne and I have had the joy of meeting people with surprising stories of their encounters with … the unexplained. The most authentic of these usually come from people who don't consider themselves very 'spiritual'. These encounters have dramatically changed their awareness and way of life.

A couple of years ago, we met Kurt and Katy down-to-earth, hard-working people. The story they shared with us was raw, unexpected, and beautifully meaningful. In the midst of unbearable physical, financial and emotional challenges, their story took a sudden turn. Not only were their eyes opened to the beauty dormant in their own lives, but also in the lives of everyone they came in touch with.

Transformed experience always goes hand-in-hand with a transformed story. In this book the text flow between their actual experiences and the way their concepts were transformed in the process. Traditional Christians might raise an eyebrow at how they subvert some cherished theological concepts, but it is difficult to argue against a transformed life.

For me, the essence of their message is that against all expectations, against all they thought religion taught, God unveiled 'Himself ' as someone much better than could ever have been anticipated. The counter-intuitive way in which this God involves Himself in our lives defies every notion getting-what-you-think-you-deserve. This God desires to give to you far more than what you believe you deserve, far more than you can contain.

Their stories have a raw honesty about them. I believe, just as I did, you find this book and easy, engaging, and exciting read.

-Andre Rabe

Author of Creative Chaos

ACKNOWLEDGEMENTS

We would like to thank our families for being with us through this journey. Our Late friend Jim Dennis who always encouraged us to write our Angel story and was a great friend for many years. To Ed and Joyce for encouraging us to share our revelations and being wonderful examples of love to us. To Debbie for letting us bend her ear on many of these topics along with being an incredible friend. To Don and Shawn for offering insight on the cover and giving us insight on marketing, as well as being our friends who always encourage and receive us despite the situations we are in. To Barbara for helping us hone in our writing skills, persuading us to add many of the testimonies that made the final copy of our book, and for being a great influence on Katy during her teenage years. To Taylor for his encouragement for us to share these thoughts and experiences in a book format. To Ray and Charlene for all the unconditional love you continue to pour out on us and for our weekly dinners when you are in town. To Mike and Barb for meeting us with Love and challenging us to live how we were designed. To Donald for making us better writers and helping us make certain the message in this book is clear.

A special thanks to Nathan for being with us for many of these testimonials and for being a good friend throughout our growth along this road of meeting God face to face as he is in our hearts.

Kurt- To Joe for listening to many of my rambling ons over the last few years as I was examining and re-examining many of the beliefs I previously held. To Sean for being someone I know has my back. To Katy for being an amazing woman who reminds me of my perfection, whom I deeply love.

Acknowledgements

Katy- To Mike and Deb for all the things you said to me years ago that now, through this writing process, I have come to understand. To Sandy for always meeting me with love and acceptance. To Julie for showing me that God is bigger than any walls or boxes people try to put him in. That perspective broke me open and allowed my heart to receive light! Lastly to Kurt for all you do daily that reminds me how perfectly I was created. Your example of love has given my heart the ability to receive love deeper and a more joyful meaning, I love you!

INTRODUCTION

When Kurt and I first began dating we briefly discussed what we thought of spiritual matters. We quickly each gave our understanding of where we were at, superficial enough that we would still date, not so in depth that if we didn't agree it would be cause to break up. We both knew quickly that we wanted to spend the rest of our lives together. However, we had no idea what that looked like and how we would make it work. We both knew that communication is key to making any relationship last. Even in knowing that, we never dug deep enough into the concepts that shape and mold who we are for fear of rejection, condemnation and ultimately opposing beliefs being the reason we couldn't be together. Maybe that sounds crazy. In todays society people of opposing beliefs don't have discussions. Let's be real. If there happens to be a disagreement arguments happen, relationships risk coming to an end and lives are forever changed. This book is the unfolding of many of our discussions on make or break topics around spiritually.

We began dating in 2005, we were married in 2010 and it wasn't until 2014 that we both got the courage to allow ourselves to be vulnerable and risk our feelings around hell, salvation, and forgiveness to name a few topics. As our trust with each other grew these discussions quickly accelerated, and have carried us on the ride of our lives. In many ways this book is about much of our eye witness accounts and experiences of our journey from darkness to light. As well as what we learned along the way.

We started writing our blog, expandingtheeyeofthestorm.com, in November of 2016. We are grateful for the many email subscribers and followers we have around the world who have continued with us and joined us through the progression of many topics and ideas we have written about. We both felt so liberated by these discussions that we felt moved to share what we were experiencing both spiritually and relationally. The blog was birthed out of that desire. We have received so many messages from people who have been relieved to find that they are not alone on their journey of questioning what they've been taught. We initially started writing this book in the fall of 2017. We had multiple starts and then totally scrapped what we had written because we didn't feel we had full enough clarity on all the topics were discussing. We are pleased to have come to the end of the road with this book. We look forward to the many discussions we will have about these topics moving forward. Our desire is not to ruffle your feathers but rather to examine and discuss things that impact each of our lives. These discussions have caused us so much freedom and allowed us to be our authentic selves. This experience has been so liberating we want others to have and share that experience.

Part One of our book is about a few of the supernatural events that happened in our lives and led us down the path we are still on today. Both of us have experienced great joy and sorrow on this path. However, in the midst of both extremes we have learned to expand the eye of the storm. In the eye of any storm is an absolute calm and peace that pushes back the barrier to protect the center from what is ragging around it. By discussing our foundational beliefs, knowing that they are not set in stone and how our experiences will evolve our understandings, we have discovered that the storms of life don't toss us around, to the depth they did in the past. This is because of the peace that we have around our spirituality.

In Part's Two and Three of this book we share things we have experienced that allowed our discussion to unfold. We invite you to have a discussion on the 11 core beliefs and/or teachings that brought us major doubt and fear. We believe these 11 core discussions could ultimately enhance your life by allowing your authenticity to be exposed. The more these are discussed by more and more people it could have a great impact on the world we live in. Relationships are a beautiful gift. By eliminating prejudgement and compartmentalizing by age, race, religion or lack of religion, barriers of separation are removed and true authentic relationships are formed. Despite prior and current beliefs.

In Part's Four and Five we discuss and share testimonies of how we can live and enjoy life in the security of both when things are going good and when things seem out of control. When people have a foundational belief they are OK and are assured they are loved, actions change. When hurting people are healed, they no longer hurt others. Love always wins out!

Our desire is to share the good news we have found living in the depths of our hearts. Since we are *all* created good the truth of our goodness flows out of our hearts when we hear how wonderfully we are made. This good news jumps for joy when we hear the truth about who we really are and who the Creator of the entire universe really is. Our path of discovery has happened in and out of Christianity. We know that everyone's path is influenced by their surroundings and all these surroundings, including Christianity have things that effect us both positively and negatively.

We sincerely hope you enjoy the discussion we continue to have with each other on these subjects: Forgiveness, Sin, Repentance and Baptism, Confession, Your Creator, The Enemy, Hell, The Lake of Fire, Salvation, and The Creator. We believe these have been the most important discussions we have ever had, and we feel it is certainly one worth having! By turning over the topics above and looking at them from all sides we have gained new perspective. Writing this book has been such a journey of growing in both of our conviction, knowing that our story is worth sharing. Religion and a healthy relationship are polar opposites. Having these discussions we share in this book has allowed us to removed religion and has created a beautiful healthy relationship to unfold in both of our lives. Our eyes have been opened as though we are children in the way we view *all* of humanity.

We ask that you take time as you read this book to ask your inner-self about what you are reading and to discuss the topics with your friends and family.

Its my experience that boldness and conviction are huge strengths and we both grew immensely in the process of finding our voice! During one of the darkest times in my life my friend Barb, who is referred to as coach in this book asked me what she could do to help me. I was deep in a dark world of using drugs to escape the pain in my soul. I said, "just continue to love me," she did and has to this day. Her and I often reflect on how impactful that statement was for both of us. Knowing we are loved unconditionally allows us to trust which ultimately allows the vulnerability we need to heal through the hurts in our lives. This book is our experience of coming into relationship with true, unconditional, unwavering love.

Many people believe that if others are told they are loved and don't need to ask for forgiveness from God that they will continue to struggle in life. There are worldly consequences for behaving certain ways. Forgiveness is beneficial to healing broken relationships and being accountable when something goes wrong. However, our experience has been the exact opposite. The more we know we are loved the more our actions and behaviors naturally change. The ugliness of religion has caused so many people unnecessary struggles. What was meant to be freeing for pain and acceptance of *all* has turned into a cesspool of condemnation, do's and don'ts turning what is suppose to be unconditional into a performance based system. Where we are the jury and God is the judge. Our ability to feel fully alive came when we walked away from the ugliness of religion and fully embraced the healthy relationship we have all been given with the Creator of all of mankind.

With love and blessings,

Katy & Kurt

TABLE OF CONTENTS

Part One

THE CATALYST
"The Start of Our Discussion"

WHAT IF?

Our Angel Experience

In the spring of 2007, Katy and I were traveling across the beautiful state of Montana, where we had just spent the night with Katy's mom in the little town of Jackson, Montana, high up in the Rocky Mountains. We got up in the morning to make the trip home to Kalispell, Montana. When we got up that morning the sun was shining. The weather quickly changed as we started driving down Lost Trail Pass, we turned the first corner and ran directly into a snowstorm. What began as dry roads immediately turned to a sheet of ice and snow. As we attempted to slow down, we slid straight off the road. Two small trees stopped our momentum, and we hung suspended at a near ninety-degree angle about ten feet below the icy road. These two small trees were the only thing keeping us from falling hundreds of feet to the valley bottom. In shock we were frozen in fear, knowing that any movement could be the end of us. Katy was able to call her mom, who, along with her husband, left their house immediately to find us.

While we were engulfed in fear and in darkness, the passenger door opened and a glowing man opened the door. He proceeded to tell us, "Don't be afraid." The next thing we both remember is standing back on the road and looking down at the truck we were driving. At this point we were in awe that we were both alive. Unless you were on the edge of the road, you could not see the vehicle. The glowing man told us he had "seen our tracks in the snow," but when we looked back at the road, so much snow had come down that by then our tracks were completely buried.

I was wearing sandals without socks. The glowing man told us his name was Mike and led us to his blue Subaru Outback to stay warm. Once inside he told us that he travels this road all the time and that he comes onto many accidents. He said, "Some people live and others die." He spoke with great peace. The amazing comfort and security Katy and I felt in his presence is something we will both vividly remember and will never forget.

2

Part One: The Catalyst

When Katy's mom came around the corner, we both got out of the warmth of Mike's vehicle. Both of us wanted to introduce Mike to Katy's mom. We were amazed when we turned around and the Subaru was gone. We asked her if she's seen the car. She shook her head and told us we were just standing on the road and there wasn't another car there.

This event began a new chapter in our lives and laid the foundation for the conviction that something was taking care of us. Yet neither of us knew the why or how we had just been saved from death. The truth is "something" supernatural was present when we thought we were going to fall to our deaths. Two trees a few inches in diameter growing on the side of a cliff stopped us in mid-air, and then a glowing Angel who said his name was Mike appeared, lifting us back up the cliff and comforting us until others arrived. For more than a decade we have often thought about this event, and every time we think about it we are overwhelmed with gratitude that two trees and an Angel came to our rescue. This memory reminds us that we matter to God and are not insignificant.

Our journey to find peace and joy in ourselves and in the world has been an incredible one. We met in the twelve-step world (Alcoholics Anonymous and Narcotics Anonymous). We thought we were broken; however, looking back on this time in our lives, nothing could have been further from the truth. We weren't broken. We weren't lost like we'd thought. We had no idea how truly loved we were, how perfectly designed we were, or how we had the perfect companions to live and enjoy life to the fullest. Neither of us had a relationship with the Father, Son, or the Holy Spirit. But in our darkness, they met us on several occasions and were in relationship with us from our beginnings, even though we were blind to their presence, compassion, affection, desire to be in a relationship with us, and ultimately their unconditional, unwavering love they have for us.

WHAT IF?

Katy's Experience

The Trinity is always there with us in and through all experiences we have in life. In fact, my first recollection was an encounter that happened when I was a young child. I remember waking up in the middle of the night and seeing a giant man covered in metal at the foot of my bed. I remember sitting in awe having a sense of peace that I had never felt before that moment. My parents and sister from that moment heard me tell them about the "metal man" and ask them questions about him. I would often get the response that "it must have been a dream." That answer never set right in my heart. The metal man glowed and was so majestic. I was not frightened or scared. I just remember a sense of peace that would come over me like I was protected. I recall many times since that event longing that I would wake up in the middle of the night and catch the metal man watching over me. I really believe that if we all reflected about times in our lives, we could account for moments where something out of the ordinary happened that gave us comfort and peace, and maybe even joy. I didn't grow up in a family where God, or spirituality was talked about. Today I am convinced that it was God igniting the echo in my heart causing me to embark on a lifelong journey of seeking exactly what it is that gives us life and gives life meaning. The echo I am speaking of is the confirmation of everything that rings as truth in our core. It is the sound the trinity makes through our heartbeat, through our senses as well as the confirmation of our emotions that we are all OK, 100 % of the time. Some of my earliest memories are of catching a glimpse of a duck floating on a pond, hearing the sounds of the birds in the distance, as well as the river outside my bedroom window. I lived a block away from the Wild Mile in Bigfork, Montana, and every spring I could sit outside or hear through the opening in my window the waters raging as though they were ignited in a battle and leading the forces to victory. Many times I would go sit by the river pondering the answers to make sense of what life is made of. I sometimes look at situations or experiences that people are going through, or that I go through myself, and I still have questions about life and its meaning. You will notice, as you continue in this book, that Kurt and my belief in the relationship with our Creator, has ignited a desire to unravel what we have been told regarding many topics like hell, salvation, and who our Creator is. The quest we have been on and the answers we have found has brought significant Peace and Joy to our being in union with Love!

From the time of the accident on Lost Trail Pass, my brain was not functioning as it had before. I was experiencing racing thoughts, bouts of seeing everything in slow motion, a constant feeling of boiling water over my brain, and a continual constant blasting sound like a gunshot had become a daily familiarity. I had had moments throughout my life where these things happened once in a while, and honestly, I thought it was just life and that this happened to everyone else too. My first recollection of experiencing slow motion happened around the age of five. I never shared what was happening with anyone because I had experienced these things throughout my life. However when all my symptoms became regular occurrence's I was a wreck. I had lost the ability to slow my mind at all. I remember at the time thinking my thoughts were a runaway train and the only solution was going to be a major derailment. Coupled with my physical symptoms and emotional struggles, I was battling with guilt and shame. I was beating myself up for not doing better in life. After diligently working on myself for more than six years, I also felt shame for all the things I had ever done wrong. In the midst of planning our wedding, the derailment happened. I felt I was at the end of myself. I was so sad, overwhelmed and tired, the doom was so much that I was contemplating suicide, which was a very scary and lonely place to be. While driving towards Holland Lake for a camping trip with friends, I began to panic. I could barely breath, my mind was racing so fast I couldn't keep any thoughts straight. I felt as though the world I was in was closing in on me and I didn't see any chance of it ever changing. Over the course of the drive, I found myself trying to get the courage to end my life by crashing my car. Barely able to breath and handle myself, I made it to Holland Lake and approached a dear friend. I confessed how dark my life felt and promised her if nothing changed over the weekend, I would go someplace safe to help me cope with my life. So I ended up spending thirty one days at the Meadows

WHAT IF?

Treatment Facility in Wickenburg, Arizona. It was what I needed at the time and I am grateful for my time there. I was diagnosed with Temporal Lobe Epilepsy, which is a chronic disorder of the nervous system characterized by recurrent, unprovoked focal seizures that originate in the temporal lobe of the brain and typically last one or two minutes. By understanding this diagnoses, certain patterns that had formed for me finally made sense. All of my life I felt like there was a movie playing in my head, vivid imagery would overtake my thoughts. The whole reason I turned to drugs and alcohol was to try to control and change that video and soundtrack that were playing in my head. My neurologist told me the temporal lobe is the audio and visual part of the brain. When I would have seizures, they would present themselves with audio and visual hallucinations. This, coupled with slow motion and scary and depressing thoughts, made me feel like I was going crazy. Several times on this journey, I would be talking with professionals, telling them how crazy I was, and they would always assure me that I was not crazy, because people who would be considered "crazy" always thought they were doing fine. What I do know today is that even in what we perceive as the darkest times of our lives, that echo is still causing us to seek and find what we all desperately long for, which is assurance and acceptance from our Creator and for our life to have purpose.

Between the middle of 2007 and August 2011, life got heavy, very overwhelming and extremely confusing for me. I was on so many medications trying to stabilize the seizures that I didn't know if I was coming or going. There were just so many things going on at one time that didn't make sense. I was suffering massive depression and still contemplating suicide. The monthly bill just for my medications was $2500, a month. The financial burden of my illness, coupled with me not being able to work weighed heavy on my confidence. Kurt did everything he could to provide for us. He took a job at a hotel as a night auditor, and he kept our painting business going during the day. He would come home and shower and nap for a few hours in the evening. I am so blessed that he was and still is my husband. I was taking twenty pills daily, just to function without experiencing seizures.

In August of 2011, we went to Colorado Springs to visit some friends. They invited us to church. Honestly, we only went that day because we wanted to spend time with them. I was always searching for the truth from the time I had the metal man experience as was Kurt. "Religion" was so ugly in our minds, and with our past experiences of being told we needed to behave a certain way to be loved by God and the legalism we viewed from church, it was the last thing we wanted or needed in our lives. However, we did want the apparent peace that our good friends Ron and Marthie had, so we joined them that Sunday morning. Marthie had become a good friend during this time in my life and she knew everything that was going on with us. Even though she lived in Colorado we spoke on the phone often, In many ways her phone calls gave me enough hope to make it through another day. After the service Marthie turned to me and simply said, "If you allow Pastor Mike to pray for you, God will heal you."

To me that sounded crazy. In my heart I longed for a miracle, but I had never seen people laying hands on other people and miracles happening. I wasn't sure about any of this at all. Kurt looked at me, and without saying a word, I saw his eyes saying to me, "What do you have to lose, we are bankrupt, buried in life, and forever seems way too long to have to live the way we are living." So, Marthie and I went to see Pastor Mike Popovich for prayer. I was terrified. This was totally new to me. I didn't know what to expect. Even though I doubted, I could be healed I was desperate, and hoped God would heal me. If I was healed, I knew my life would change. I badly wanted this to happen, but still I wasn't sure. Yet, Marthie's confidence was attractive and I trusted her just enough to allow Pastor Mike to pray for me.

After a brief intro with the pastor, he asked me to fill him in on what I was struggling with. I told him the sanitized version, which was still pretty dark. Seizures, hopelessness, depression, suicidal and scared thoughts ruled my life. He looked at me with confidence and said something like, "Oh that's nothing for God. Easy." I got irritated. I remember thinking, "Easy, you jerk? It is a daily struggle to get out of bed!" I considered it a successful day if I got to the shower and back into bed. Easy? Suicide was still on my mind at this point, and the frickin medication I was on for my seizures had ballooned me up from 170 pounds to 340 pounds. Easy? He has no idea what it was like to live in my head, let alone do that and try to function well for a few hours. However, I stayed. He said a quick prayer while he was anointing me with oil. At the time I didn't feel different from the prayer and oil. I walked out of that church, went to take my medication, which was a two time a day routine with ten pills. Immediately after being prayed over, I threw up the medication, which is something that had never happened before. This continued every day after I took it.

To this day I have never had another seizure, and I don't take the medication anymore. My life was transformed in an instant that day. Before this healing, I was experiencing five to eight seizures a month. I was so heavily medicated that friends and family thought they'd lost me, since I was unable to really interact with anyone. Not too long ago, Marthie told me that my demeanor changed from her seeing me as an empty shell to having an ignited spark of life in my eyes within moments of Mike praying for me.

Kurt's Experience

After Katy was prayed for, we talked a little bit with a few people and then made our way out of the building. Immediately I noticed this majestic tree that I hadn't seen when we pulled into the parking lot. Peace swept over me and seemed to boil out of every part of my being. My heart cried out: "God created all of the world and is bigger than any illness people have." Hallelujah! This outburst from my heart brought me to tears. I was overcome with joy. Just thinking back on this wonderful day and how it has forever changed our lives still moves me. Our lives took a complete turn for the better. The tree I see in my mind is how I visualize the tree of life big, beautiful, healthy, and inviting. Hearty enough to give us shade and protect us from all storms. A tree to have a picnic under. The next time I visit Colorado Springs, I want to go back to that parking lot and see if there really is a tree there or if it was the Spirit living in me, sharing the Father's love and the Tree of Life with me.

Katy and I began sharing this event with everyone who had ears to hear. A few months later we got a call from a friend, who asked us if we would come to her house and pray for her aunt who had a severe eye infection. She told us the doctors believed she was going to lose her eyesight. Neither of us knew anything about praying for other people, so we searched for a few scriptures to read. We also stopped at the grocery store to get some olive oil, since Katy was healed, after the pastor put olive oil on her.

When we arrived at the house, we said a short prayer in the car and then went in. We told the aunt about Katy being healed, poured some oil on our hands, put them on her head, read By His wounds you have been healed. (-1 Peter 2:21) Such a prayer offered in faith will heal the sick, and the Lord will make you well. (-James 5:15) and closed with In Jesus name we pray. These were just scriptures we had found Googling on the way over to her house, because we knew nothing about praying for anyone or even praying for ourselves at this time in our life. The aunt then told us how hot the oil had gotten on the side of her head. This seemed like proof that something was happening. It was really a quick in and out. Our prayer wasn't long, the conversation only lasted a few minutes. We didn't have any previous experience to go by, except Katy being healed. She thanked us as we left. On the way home both of us thought maybe we should go back and put oil on her infected eye since maybe we put it in the wrong spot.

The next day we got a call from our friend and her aunt. They told us the infection had miraculously disappeared. All we could do was laugh, because at that moment we knew two things: we didn't heal her but God did. From that day forward, we have seen more then a hundred people healed from every ailment you can imagine. As you read this book many parts ahead we'll tell of events and miracles that have led to our re-examining many subjects and changed many of the beliefs we previously held. The journey for you lies in your life, and we believe this book will help you live victorious on every path you take.

9

Moving forward in this book we will share our adventure of dissecting and re-examining fifteen topics that deal with issues like baptism, confession and forgiveness that have caused us both great confusion and doubt. We believe there is great value in examining their context and the ramifications of a distorted viewpoint.

We certainly don't claim to have all the answers to your questions, but we believe there are some foundational truths about who we are, who we have always been, and who we will always be that must be shared. When these truths are cultivated from the depths of your heart, you will begin to experience the life and peacefulness you have always desired – The life God has designed for you from the beginning! Life was meant to be enjoyed not endured.

In the depths of your heart the Spirit of God is alive and well. He will let you know if this is the truth that can change your life as it resonates within you. In the book of Genesis, we read about how Adam and Eve are enticed to eat something that would make them more like God. After they eat it, they are filled with guilt, shame and unworthiness. When God finds them attempting to hide from him because they thought they think they have disappointed Him, He asks them, "Who told you that?" What God was asking is who told you that you aren't perfect just the way you are, and who told you that you are a disappointment to me? These two lies we hear are essentially the basis for all issues we have and experience in life. If we never thought we were not perfect, we wouldn't spend so long trying to become something we aren't.

The good news is, if you are looking to be free of physical illness, stress, anxiety, eating disorders, drug addiction, alcoholism, or any kind of addiction, or if you are looking to have more financial security and success in your life, or if you are looking to have deeper, more loving relationships, we believe this book will benefit you.

Along this journey you likely will read viewpoints that are totally new to you , but we ask that you take them to your heart by asking, *"What if this is the truth that will set me free?"* Your heart will always rejoice in the truth of who God really is and who you really are and have been created to be.

So, put your seatbelt on, check your rear view mirrors, take pit stops at the end of each topic to examine what you have just read, have discussions with your friends and family. But most importantly enjoy the ride...............

Part Two

THE GOAT

"The Greatest of All Time"

WHAT IF?

Our Experience

Several years ago, we started having a fellowship gathering at our house. Neither Katy nor I had extensive Bible knowledge. We both knew the basic stories and had been listening to sermons regularly for several months. I grew up going to church sporadically as a child, whereas Katy went with family friends as a child and then a few times before she was miraculously healed.

When we started our fellowships, both of us felt like we were chartering new territory and didn't want to steer anyone in the wrong direction. While we were visiting with friends and Pastor Mike Popovich in Minneapolis, I expressed our concerns that we didn't know the Bible as well as others, due to the fact that several people called us baby christians. Pastor Mike tapped me on the chest and said, "God has placed the word on your heart, and the Bible will support what comes out of your heart." From that moment on, if I had a thought about who God really was and how He sees us, Katy and I would "Google" certain topics and ideas and bam, there would be scriptures to support it.

The further we got on this journey the more truth was being revealed in our heart with echoes of joy and peace. Katy started a weekly Bible study over the phone with a friend. She immediately noticed how the New King James Version she was using was very different in context than the New International Version her friend was using. She began to check other versions of the Bible we downloaded on a Bible App. Each of the translations had some similarities. However, some verses weren't included in all the translations, and some verses had a completely different meaning or interpretation from one another.

This discrepancy caused us to wonder which version was the closest to the original scripture. Whether it's in the Old Testament or the New Testament, there are many versions of scripture and many times there's a big differences in meaning.

The Greek word for *Gospel* is *Euaggelion*, which means "too good to be true."

The word *euaggelion* had never been used before Jesus told the disciples after He had come back from the dead to "Go into the world and proclaim the Gospel to all of Creation." (- Mark 16:15) The word *gospel* by its true meaning defies logic. How can something really be too good to be true?

When we learned this, we began to examine each scripture in the New Testament to this standard: Is it too good to be true? Or is it only good if we must do something to make it good? We would ask ourselves "How does it feel in our hearts? If the answer we wasn't reassuring, then we would begin to investigate what original Greek or Hebrew had been. This was often tiresome and took hours of study and research. But due to the vast information available online, whether it be commentary such as, *Strong's Concordance, Young's Literal Translation*, or YouTube videos from teachers, authors, pastors, and theologians, we often found what felt true in our hearts.

As with most Christians. We have often heard how the Bible is the "inerrant word of God," scripture is infallible because the Bible is inspired by God and written through man. This sounded good for many years in our lives... but the more we realized that the "character and personality" of Jesus is the same as the Father, the more we began to see great contradictions in scripture. If God is love, then how can he choose to torture some for lack of belief while save others because they said the right words? These contradictions were evident by this vast difference in translations. Our journey into the original Greek and Hebrew languages that the original letters, stories, and songs were written in opened our eyes.

15

For example, the word that was translated as *wait* in *Isaiah 40:31* is the word *qavah* Hebrew definition is intertwined making the verse read and mean something totally different then when its been translated using the word wait. "Those who wait upon the Lord shall renew their strength; they shall mount up with wings as eagles; they shall run, and not be weary; and they shall walk, and not faint." But when *qavah* is translated as intertwined. It reads "those who are intertwined with the Lord will have strength, they will mount up with wings as eagles; they will run and not be weary; and will walk and not faint." Present tense is important to notice, because, we will explain later, everyone is intertwined in with the Father, Son, and Spirit.

These two simple words, when translated properly, relate a totally different story. They explain much of what we believe about our original design and permanent relationship with God with so much more clarity. You don't have to sit around *waiting* when you are already *intertwined* with God! Everything that has breath is connected to God.

The more we have learned about the origins of the Old Testament, the more we are reminded of the danger in childhood teachings called the "telephone game." I whisper something to my neighbor, who is supposed to whisper the same thing to their neighbor and so on and so forth. In that, the words and meaning change from the original words that were whispered or spoken. After we studied much of the history of how the Bible was put together, we saw where the telephone game came into play. The more times the story is told, the further it gets from its original truth and appears to become someone's opinion and written down from their perspective. Most of the Old Testament was passed on from generation to generation orally, often many times for many centuries before it was written down.

Most New Testament translations come from the Latin Vulgate, rather than the original letters written by Paul, John, Peter, James and Jude. The Vulgate is the letters translated from Greek into Latin for the early Catholic Church. The First Latin Vulgate was composed by St. Augustine and then as St. Jerome gained power he revamped it in 362 to fit his ideology. Both Augustine and Jerome had been greatly influenced by the philosophers of their time such as Plato. The interesting thing about both of the first two Vulgate's is neither Augustine or Jerome could read Greek. Augustine composed the New Testament from others translating orally in Latin what they were reading in Greek. Then Augustine would write what they were telling him in Latin. Jerome didn't like parts of Augustine's translation because it didn't endorse enough of Plato's belief that God was separate from his creation and viewed as an angry man perched on top of mountain who desired to punish certain souls for eternity unless they proved their worth. Jerome also didn't feel the God of the Old Testament stories was evident and alive enough in Augustine's translations. Plato's philosophy and the Jewish belief that man is separate from God had crept its way back into the Letters of the Apostles. Over the next 1,000 years, the Catholic Church continued to have new composers update the Latin vulgate to fit into this belief and also to make certain that particular scriptures promoted the entire well being of the entire church, including the finances to keep expanding their vast network of churches.

This belief about God is doesn't line up with the how the church viewed God before roughly 500 AD. But it got enough steam over the decades to have major influence on Christianity and the Muslim faith. This new idea that some people go to hell, others to purgatory, and a select few go to paradise is a direct contradiction to the character of God the Father, the Holy Spirit, and Jesus. This is what Paul warned the none, Jewish audience about in *Colossians 2:8-9,* when he wrote "Make sure that you become no

17

one's victim through empty philosophical intellectualism and meaningless speculations, molded in traditions and repetitions according to mankind's cosmic codes and superstitions and not consistent with Christ. (Any teaching that leaves you with a sense of lack and imperfection rather than completeness is a distraction from the truth.) It is in Christ that God finds an accurate and complete expression of himself, in a human body!" -Mirror Bible

The King James Version of the Bible came in the time often referred to as the Reformation period. The first completed translation of the New Testament written in English was believed to be the Tyndale Bible, and the first printed English version of the Bible was the Coverdale Bible in 1535. The King James Version was completed in 1604 and began printing in 1611. All of the Bible's during this time leaned heavily on the Latin Vulgate and the English translations before them to compose the New Testament, because the translators were often fluent in Hebrew, Aramaic, Latin, and English and had little to no understanding of Greek, since the majority of the translators were educated by the Catholic Church, which did not teach Greek to their monks or priests.

Along the way, new verses were added, others were taken out, and most theologians agree that at least twenty-five New Testament scriptures have either been added or taken out. Because of different views about the character of God the Father, the Holy Spirit, and Jesus Christ, the content of the original letters has drifted further and further from the original context and towards the belief of the writers of the New Testament.

We are often told not to take everything at face value and "that if it didn't come straight from the horse's mouth, we need to be careful." So, whose mouth is each Bible translation coming from? A few years ago, we were in the process of re-translating a few verses in the New Testament and had even written multiple blogs where we explained what our take on certain verses were and many times we retranslated the verses after hours and hours of study.

Then we got exposed to the Mirror Bible, which to this date is only about 95% of the New Testament starting with the Book of Luke. This translation is being done by Francois du Toit who is a scholar of the Greek language, translator and teacher of early church history. Immediately we fell in love with the Mirror Bible, because when we looked up a few of the verses we had diligently re-translated for blogs we had written, found our translations matched his translations.

What we have learned from listening to many talks on YouTube from Francois Du Toit is that he has a great understanding of the character of God and how God sees his creation. Francois originally translated a few of the epistles in the mid 1980's and began working on translating the entire New Testament in 2007. Francois told us that eventually the entire New Testament will be translated and also five books of the Old Testament. We highly recommend the Mirror Bible and are personally excited about his future translations. We endorse it to anyone who wants to hear what the heart of God says about them. Most of the Bible scriptures we reference are from the Mirror Bible.

All translations, even the Mirror Bible, are skewed to some degree to fit the theology they have been influenced by. But what we love about the Mirror Bible translation is when we read it, we hear the Spirit living inside us echo the words as we read them and affirm that this is the Good News of who God is. How God sees us and how much He loves and adores us. It shows us clearly how God sees us and how wonderfully we all have been created.

In many of the conversations the two of us have we start with "What if ?" Why is it we are taught the Golden Rule as kids, which is to treat others as you want to be treated. We were taught to not only listen to others but learn for ourselves. But then when we get into a religious environment, we are told to listen to the authorities and that what they say about God is true. We are told if our hearts don't resonate with scripture, then we need to cleanse our heart. We are told that *all* are born with the sinful nature of Adam, but then we are taught that only some will be saved by Jesus. Depending on different theologies, some are predetermined to be saved, others earn their way to heaven by numerous ways, including works or by confessing Jesus is lord. We are told that every word of the Bible is inspired and the written word of God. However, every denomination puts their own spin on it. They claim that we need to live by the Golden Rule, but often preach the opposite of how Jesus himself lived while on earth. Jesus loved everyone but some congregations kick out people living together out of wedlock or are in a same sex relationship.

The Golden Rule is the principle of treating others as oneself would wish to be treated. Yet many denominations have issues with people who don't live up to what they think God wants them to live up to.

Our Experience

A young man who we have had the pleasure of getting to know over the last few years told us that when he was younger his family went to a church for a little while, but then when each of his older brothers showed up wearing earrings the pastor blasted them and told them that homosexuals were not allowed in his church. Unless they took their earrings out, they were not to come back. Now, these were just two teenage boys who, like everyone else, needed to know that the creator of all mankind loved them, yet this pastor apparently doesn't believe God loves everyone.

Our eyes of understanding began to open to the truth that God is love and that if scripture doesn't support this then it is not a true reflection of God. Katy and I remember feeling liberated. We both recall when doubts we had were lifted off of us and we quit walking around only half informed. Once we began to trust that our hearts actually had the truth in them all along, and we began to live "intertwined" rather than "waiting," our vision began to lose the blur of ignorance and ego and we began to feel more at peace than any other time in our lives. We began trusting that *all* means *all* for everyone rather than *all* meaning *all* for Adam, but only some for Jesus. The word *reconciliation* took so much more meaning and is now completely freeing and totally uplifting.

The reason we are sharing our new understandings is because we have found freedom in the Love of the God who has created us in His image and likeliness. If you don't agree with us, that's OK. We are not saying, "We are right and you are wrong." We are saying this is what is true for us, and this truth completely altered our life, and in this truth we have found peace and joy that has surpassed anything we thought was possible.

Our desire is for everyone reading this book to dive deep into your own heart and to have the discussion between you and your creator, yourself and other people. Re-examine your inner truths, not only on the topics we have written about. But also on the topics that seem to be in conflict with what your heart echoes to be true. Any topic that causes your heart to feel sickened or pained would be good to examine. When clarity and peace come that is the echo confirming truth. This book is our encouragement for everyone to re-examine what you may have been taught from churches, mentors, and how we have viewed personal experiences we have had with others and for you to engage in a conversation with your Maker. We believe that we all have questions that arise with things that have been and are being told to us. Most of the questions resulted for us when we heard God is love but. Sadly, when we are told we need to act a certain way to be pleasing to God, by people of influence, we condemn, and silently shame ourselves, if what they say doesn't sit well with our hearts. Both of us spent most of our lives living that way. Because many of these topics never resonated in our hearts we both desperately wanted to talk about the questions we had about God and the view He had of all of mankind. But we didn't begin to examine this until we were exposed to teachers, theologians, translators, and author's such as Dr. C. Baxter Kruger, Mike and Barb Popovich, Francois Du Toit, Don Keathley, Wm. Paul Young, and Andre and Mary-Ann Rabe to name a few. Even though we don't always agree with their take on the topics they write or talk about. Their courage and willingness to cover subjects that we had often questioned allowed us to examine God for ourselves, and when we finally saw ourselves as intertwined and in seamless union with a God that we see as a Triune God, we had the confidence to talk about all the things which we had previously questioned with others. The beautiful thing about union is that we can now pose the questions and trust that the relationship we have with the trinity will unfold and disclose what we are now open to hear.

The answer to a big question that we always thought about but felt guilty for thinking about we found in the book of John: "In the beginning was the Word, and the Word was with God, and the Word was God. He was in the beginning with God. All things were made through Him, and without Him nothing was made that was made. In Him was life, and the life was the light of men. And the light shines in the darkness, and the darkness did not comprehend it."(-John 1:1-5 NKJV)

We never understood that if Jesus was the Word and in the beginning with God, and the Bible is also the inerrant word of God and all scriptures come from God, then why do most scriptures portray Jesus as loving and accepting and God as vengeful, angry, and just in the Old Testament stories? This contradiction between the personality of Jesus and the personality of God has caused much strife. When Jesus clearly said, *"If you have seen me then you have seen the Father." (-John 14:9).* Jesus affirms his unity with the Father. The first time we read this we felt great freedom. And the two of us have had many conversations about this simple subject.

The more research we have done on the topic and the belief that the word of God is without error, the clearer we saw the Word is Jesus, and Jesus is Love. The more obvious it became that The Word is *not* the Bible, and that the Old Testament has many stories that do not represent God and are in conflict with the God we have met. The story of Love is evident in all translations of the books Matthew, Mark, Luke, and John. We now clearly see how Jesus told teachers of the Old Testament that they didn't know God. Even though He was standing directly in front of them (-John 14:9), they didn't recognize him. He referred to all the teachers of the Old Testament as "hypocrites and sons of the devil." (-Matthew 23:13-15) It is now evident to us that the character and nature of Jesus is in many ways, the complete opposite of Gods character we read about in the Old Testament. But as we mentioned, Jesus said, *"If you have seen me you have seen the Father." (-John 14:9)* The Apostle Paul also wrote that God is the same yesterday, today, and tomorrow, that His character does not change. (*-Hebrews 13:8)*

Since Jesus healed everyone he came in contact with and showered His unconditional love on those whom others thought were dirty, then so does the Father and the Holy Spirit. This is an amazing truth about who God the Father is, who the Holy Spirit is, and who Jesus is.

What we began to see was that when we filter what we have been taught through the church verses common sense and humility, a great conversation begins to happen. We no longer have to follow the idea that we need to save people. Now we are able to meet people with the love we have found in God. This shift from the legalism of religion into the love and acceptance for *all* has been wonderful.

We have approached many of these ideas we from the "*What if?*" perspective for the last several years, and it has been quite an amazing journey. This has allowed us to look at many sides of scripture and then to allow the echo within "the Word" to confirm the truth, because it is in His breath which gives *all* things life. Everyone has His spirit (the Word) living inside of them that will sing in glory when we hear the truth of who we really are and who we have always been. *All* things were made by Him and He dwells in everything.

What Pastor Mike said years ago is true for everyone: "God has placed the word in your heart, and the Bible will support what comes out of your heart." Also, if what you are reading about God in the Bible or what you are being taught doesn't cause your heart to leap with joy, then it is not the truth about who you are, who God is, and certainly not the Word of God.

The echo we each have in our hearts has gotten louder the more we discover truths that we had never heard before. The "Word" is alive and the inerrant word of God lives in all of us. The word is talked about and explained in many parts of the Bible and in all translations, but the word is not the Bible. The Word lives in all of mankind, and glimpses are found in all belief 's and practices around the globe. We believe the Word will never leave you or forsake you. The Word echoes the good news of how wonderfully and perfectly you have been made. The Word lifts you up when you are feeling down. For us we see, the Word as Jesus, but more importantly, the Word is Love. The Word is the foundation of who we are. The Word loves us, laughs with us, encourages us, and assures us of how much we are really liked and really truly loved.

"The fact that you are a Christ-Epistle shines as bright as day! This is what our ministry is all about. The Spirit of God is the living ink. Every trace of the Spirit's influence on the heart is what gives permanence to this conversation. We are not talking law-language here; this is more dynamic and permanent than letters chiseled in stone. This conversation is embroidered in your inner consciousness." (-2 Corinthians 3:3 Mirror Bible)

What if, the word is all humanity? What if, the Word lives in everyone and echoes the truth about who we all are and who God is?

Part Three

TEN ELEPHANTS IN
THE ROOM

When Katy was healed, we started to go to a local church, where we joined a small group and attempted to do everything the church asked of us. We began to listen to only Christian music and watch only Christian-approved movies. Things seemed to be OK, although we didn't enjoy this way of life. Even though by "certain standards" we were saved, our outlook was, "Who needs to have peace and joy as long as we were going to go to heaven?"

The church we were attending, quickly looked dead. We saw frustration and fear on the faces in the small group we attended and at the weekly church service. Where was the joy? Most of the people appeared to be just going through the motions. We knew this was not the life we wanted. Then, while we were traveling for business, we met with Pastor Mike Popovich and his wife, Barb, in Portland, Oregon. They told us if we wanted to start something with them in Kalispell, Montana, they would fly in every few months to help get it off the ground. We thought, "Why not?" They were sharing a message we didn't think was being shared in our hometown.

Immediately we began to see miracle after miracle at our weekly fellowships. It was exciting, and we began to experience joy. We didn't know what was going to happen next, but we knew it it would be amazing, and in most cases something miraculous. Mike and Barb came up occasionally, but the majority of the time we led the small group with the help and guidance of the Holy Spirit.

For the past several years, we have met with a group of people weekly or bi-weekly weekly. What we have experienced over the years has been nothing short of wonderful. We have seen people's lives change as they began to experience freedom from the bondage religion had produced in their lives. The group, like all groups, has ebbed and flowed. Some of the faces have changed. People have moved out of the area or spent their time elsewhere.

The first year went smoothly. We tuned into Mike Popovich's sermons on line @FreedomMinistries.org. We would discuss many of the topics Pastor Mike was sharing at our fellowship, and spend time in prayer and worship. We now see that we became sort of addicted to the rush of the miraculous, but the joy we first had when we saw miracles quickly turned to chasing the miracles. Looking back at that time we can now see how bound we were, because we didn't want to disappoint God by not being available twenty four hours a day when people called.

What started with us seeing miracle after miracle, eventually opened our eyes to the concept that God the Father is good, loves us, and wants to provide for us. We were beginning to see that God's character and personality is the same as Jesus and Holy Spirit. We realized that *all* three are good, unconditionally love us, and want to provide for us. During that time in our life, we believed this was only if we accepted Jesus as our savior. But what if the Trinity has loved everyone from the foundation of the world?

As our understanding grew, we were exposed to Joseph Prince. Joseph's messages were completely new to us. We began to hear what is called the "Grace Message" and it hit us like a ton of bricks. Our hearts leapt for joy, but our brains couldn't believe the Gospel could be this good. This revelation knocked us down, but we got back up as this deeper message of love elevated us to a new understanding of who God is and how He sees us. Over the years, our understanding has grown beyond Joseph Prince, but we realize he was a good starting point for us.

WHAT IF?

We now realize the Gospel of Grace is in many ways a contradiction to mainstream Christianity, but is very is the similar to message the Apostle Paul wrote about in his letters in the New Testament. For us, the message of Grace was the catalyst to many of the "What If 's" we began to examine in the Bible and in our hearts. At first this teaching was hard to believe. But our hearts began to leap with peace and joy. We thought, "How could God really love us unconditionally, when our entire lives we had been taught God only showers some with His love? How could He really see us as perfect, even when we mess up or don't act the way the church suggests we act? Our hearts are now certain this is the too good to be true news that Jesus told his disciples to proclaim to the entire world. (-Mark 16:15)

You may be thinking, "What if this is really true? Does God only have love and kindness for mankind?" For us, these questions and many more overwhelmed our minds, but our hearts leap with joy and peace every time we discover the truth. This has sent us down what others call the Grace Road...

In this part we are going to discuss what we consider the ten big elephants in the room of religious teaching. We realize that you, like us, might initially struggle mentally with most of these topic, but we believe the freedom we found in re-examining these topics is contagious. Because, the Gospel is by the undiluted definition always too good to be true news for *everyone*.

For us, when we realized the Word of God is written on our hearts, what we had previously been taught about on these ten topics began to unravel.

In the next several pages we are going to address what we see as elephants in the room of religion that have caused us each much fear, doubt, and insecurity. What we found in studying and discussing what we thought were foundational truths was that the truth was far from what we believed. This is part of our journey along the Grace road. Most of these topics have been foundational to most religions in the world. However, what we have discovered is when we shine love on them, our perception and reality is changed.

One

FORGIVENESS

Time and time again we have heard excuses and passing blame for personal failures on Adam and Eve's fall. They receive blame for everything negative that happens in our world. In the past we often discussed *"If the apple wouldn't have gotten eaten, then this wouldn't be the outcome."* We had heard others speak these empty words for the entirety of our lives, and we had also uttered them ourselves. They are just that... empty. They have been blamed for so long that people have begun to believe them as truth. Today we don't believe mankind has fallen because of Adam and Eve, we also don't believe mankind ever fell from the creator of the world, who is also the lover of the world.

Often we are told, "We are alive in Christ, but we are forever under the fall of Adam and Eve. Even though Jesus was resurrected, and in His resurrection we should be reminded about our true identity, instead we are often still focused on what we believe has been wrong with us for our entire life. No one needs forgiveness from a God who sees everyone as his perfect masterpiece.

As you continue to read this book, you may experience a few heart checks. What we are saying is there may be times that your heart leaps with joy, but your mind scrambles at the idea because it is so different than anything you have ever heard.

Our hope is that you are awakened to the freedom in what we are sharing. When we began to talk to God with an attitude of *"What if ?"* and "Could this really be true?" Our hearts began to heal from the hurt that had consumed us most of our lives. His resurrection and life now flows like rivers of living water into every thought and situation in our life.

"I want to say it with such clarity that no one will be able to lead you to an inferior conclusion by bending your mind with clever words." (-Colossians 2:4 Mirror Bible)

A good example of how the Old Testament is filled with stories written in an attempt to explain who God is, can be seen in Genesis 1 and 2. Genesis 1 tells us how God created the sun, the moon, the creatures of the ocean, the birds, the animals, and every creature living in the water or on the land before He created humans both male and female and told them "Be fruitful and multiply" (-Genesis 1:28). Then Genesis 2 tells us that God created the man from dust and then realized the man shouldn't be alone so he created a woman to be his helper out of the man's rib. These two stories came from two different tribes of the Jewish population. One depicts woman as equal to man and one depicts woman as less than.

The book of Genesis is not a science manual but rather a collection of great stories written by men and women in an attempt to understand a God they didn't understand. This change of how we see the story of Creation in the bible has helped us immensely. Both of these stories were written and told thousands of years ago in a attempt to explain who God is and how people came to be.

This gave us the ability to begin to see that maybe Adam and Eve is a story of us. Growing up, leaving our nest, and experiencing life.

WHAT IF?

What if, God doesn't kick us out of the home he designed for us? What if, God allows us to experience the joys and tribulations of life if we allow ourselves.

The great news is you were never lost in Adam's deeds you have always been engulfed in your Creator's love! Everything begins and ends in Him. If our genesis really came from the beginning and all things are made through Him, then why, if God is love, would he not just love us fully? Why would he continue to allow things of this world, and the idea we have fallen with Adam, dictate our experience in the here and now? The reason we walk you through this is because we ourselves needed to walk through it to come to really understand our full and beautiful dwelling in truth.

With this topic and every topic and page in this book, we ask that you set aside what you have been told and have held strongly as fact and dig into your heart to feel and see who you have always been, God's masterpiece! His perfect creation. The apple of His eye.

What is in your heart will come out! It may be shocking for some to realize that at the base of all of our thinking is where Truth lies and life begins. Our hearts and minds is what produces peace and joy. Many times we hear people say, "The journey from our head to our heart is only eighteen inches." But for both of us, this has been one of the longest and most rewarding walks we have ever taken.

The Apostle Paul wrote to the Ephesians, in Chapter 1, that he prayed for their spiritual eyes of understanding to be opened and for their spiritual ears to hear. We also pray that you hear the truth in what we share, and if something doesn't ring true, that you, continue reading and examine it again in the future.

You may even ask yourself "What if ?" and "Could this really be true?"

Things we see on TV, news, media and from other people's experiences have greatly influenced our intellectual knowledge. However, our heart knowledge was, and always has been, from the beginning with God. Out of His breath all things are made. He is in and through everything, and all that was made was made by him.

From the foundation of the world, the Spirit has lived in your heart. The Spirit edifies who you are and gives us hope in dark situations. She shines the light of who you truly are and darkness is expelled. Our righteousness is who we have always been. We are all reflections of God. Let's celebrate this and forget the distorted vision of who we "think" God is. God is *love* and *love* keeps no record of wrongs.

We are not under the fall of Adam but live and reside in the love out of which we were created! "What if " in this love we need no forgiveness from our maker!

What if, we all are perfectly created, and no one is born dirty?

Two

SIN

Most Christians are taught "sin" is inherited from Adam, that all are born sinful, and that sin is defined by nearly all religions as "an immoral act considered to be a transgression against Divine law." Much of the Christian doctrine teaches that certain transgressions are unpardonable regardless of whether or not you accept Jesus as your Savior. Others believe Jesus covered all your sins as long as you believe in His death and resurrection. We both believe in the death and resurrection of our husband and Savior Jesus Christ. But we also believe *all* are embraced forever by the Love and Glory of God.

This switch in our belief system came slowly over multiple years. When the "Aha" moment overtook our hearts, we both felt more peace around the topic of death and our mission to share the Good News than we had ever dreamt was possible. As the mental veils began to lift in our personal lives, we began to understand that *"This is final: I have deleted the record of your sins and misdeeds. It is not possible to recall them." (-Hebrews 10:17 Mirror Bible)* In past years we learned that sin had been translated from the Greek word *hamartia* which has been (and is still being) taught by many to mean "to miss the mark."

Through study, we have found that what it has nothing to do with action or behavior. *Hamartia* means "wrong belief about how God sees us"

We see it like this: Jesus came to bring his bride (*all of mankind*) out of the darkness caused by viewing ourselves and God in the wrong light. Believing we are separated from God the Creator. Recently we were listening to an interview with theologian Dr. C. Baxter Kruger, who defined sin as "not believing what Jesus says about how the Father views us". We had to listen to it a few times, and wow! Sin is any wrong belief about how God sees us." Sin isn't something we do or a the lifestyle we live. Sin is *not* an action. Sin is simply any wrong belief about how God sees us!

How does God see us? He sees us as His masterpiece. He sees us as His favorite child. He sees us just the way you are....*perfect*! No lawless deed, no mess up will ever change His feelings about you. The other day we heard a gentleman talk about how his godson was a big disappointment to himself and the son's dad. But let's not get confused with worldly views. Nothing we do can or will ever disappoint God. He doesn't see anything but how perfect we are. He is not disappointed with we for anything. Nothing can change the good news of who we are to Him.

We are born out of love and will always remain in love. We are all destined to spend eternity in the light of God. Adam and Eve had wrong beliefs about who they were, but no one is born believing they need to do something to please God. This belief comes from the influence of others. Recently we were talking to a young man who believes children are born bad. His belief is what he was taught, or possibly told, growing up.

37

If we are told how disappointed the Father is with us, that is not from the Spirit. The Spirit only echoes the truth of who we are in Her eyes, our husband's eyes, and our Father's eyes. And the truth is we are perfect just the way we are. We are perfect if we struggle with addictions. We are perfect if we are in an intimate relationship with someone of the same sex. We are perfect if we laugh at what is defined as a "dirty joke." We are perfect... period! Knowing how perfect we are will set us free from anything holding us back from enjoying life to the fullest. As Author and teacher Wm. Paul Young says, "Papa is especially fond of us!".

We are God's dream come true.

Experiencing the freedom we *all* have in union with our I-am-ness fills our hearts with unspeakable joy. Our lives mirror every aspect of the trinity. Our smiles, our bright life filled eyes and our gentle outpouring of love radiates this truth. We are the one the Shepherd left His 99 to find. We are in perfect union with the Trinity

Katy's Experience

I received a phone call from a friend's mom. I was nineteen or twenty at the time and had been on a quest of trying to figure out my life.LOL The reason for that LOL is I know understanding it is a wild adventure and that we never get it fully figured out. I really believe this process is where joy comes from. I remember thinking it was quite odd that a old high school friends mom asked me to lunch, especially since I had not spent much time with this friend since high school. I agreed to meet her and, in all honesty, I thought I could boast to her about how well I was doing in my life. I had maintained sobriety; I was taking classes at Flathead Valley Community College. I was young and truthfully had no confidence, I was looking for accolades to carry me through all the crazy turns my life was taking. If I had confidence,

I would have boasted to her. I would have used my voice and been able to show that I was confident. If I would have had confidence, maybe I could have pushed back where this encounter went. But I remained silent.

I walked into the coffee shop, tense, overwhelmed and unsure of how this was going to go. She and I had been through so many interesting encounters as I was growing up that I just told myself to chalk it up as another AFGO (another fucking growth opportunity). I had to have that perspective, otherwise I would have never shown up in the first place. We sat down and I could feel the tension.

She shared her heart with me. However, she felt that I had slandered and sinned against her family. I shut down completely. Condemnation is a silent killer. I left that meeting feeling horrible. I remember thinking that if that is what it looks like to be a Christian, I don't want anything to do with it. At the time, she asked me to get together but I had no idea why? I found out later that day that it resulted from a talk I had with a friend , in confidence, about this woman's son and my relationship. I shared some concerns that I had, but if I would have known this person I spoke to was going to call another friend and share everything I had said, I would have never talked about this stuff in the first place. However, sometimes learning things the hard way is the best way to grow. That is exactly what happened to me. I should have never opened up and trusted however, if I hadn't, then I would have never grown to understand that some things are best left unsaid.

We all have experienced times in our lives when we probably said or did something that in someone's eyes was "wrong." We are all entitled to our opinions, but, I won't take people to lunch to tell them where they are wrong. Because I know we are all on this adventure together. I am so blessed that today I have a understanding that "sin" is not an action. If sin was an action, then all of mankind would be in a vicious cycle of condemnation and unworthiness. What I learned from this encounter was a lesson for sure. But I was not a "sinner." I learned that I was a human who lacked judgement at a difficult time in my life, spoke about some things that were happening around me. Period. My whole life I have been told that sin is an action if you swear, have a bad thought, have a bad behavior. What I have come to understand through this journey of examining my heart and my relationship with the Creator is simple: If Jesus really came to take away the "sin" of the world and it's an action, then He failed plain and simple. Yes, I really just said that. If that is what he came to do, then 2,000, plus years ago the world would have been bright-eyed and guilt free and it would have remained that way through eternity. As we have referenced before, "sin" or "hamartia," is not an action. It is a belief. Having a distorted belief about how we are seen by God, distorted beliefs and views are where all shame and guilt manifest. In turn, causing all the insanity we see going on presently and throughout the history of the world. For several years this situation bothered me deeply., until in my walk of coming to know and understand the Creator I had the following revelation, that "sin" is not an action rather a distorted belief about how God sees us and we see Him.

I can remember instances throughout my life where I had said things to people or about people, as well as behaved poorly that I am not proud of, and because of what I had been taught and believed about sin I struggled with guilt, shame and condemnation. In fact, during the more insecure times in my life, these small situations festered into huge isolation events with my family, my friends, and Kurt. Having the assurance in my heart today and doing my best to see myself the way that God sees me, and loving myself in the midst of my AFGO's, I have less desire for accolades and ego and more desire for loving, meaningful relationships with depth. Once my heart changed, my life became much fuller with humanity. There is no separation from our union with God, except the distorted belief we may have about whatever we are finding fault with in ourselves. I can laugh now, knowing that I was just targeted for some inward pain and distorted thinking that lady had that day, on any other given day someone could have invited her to lunch and pulled the same cards she pulled on me. No one is any better or any worse, we are all Gods children. No one. We are all just people trying to experience our lives the best we know how. In that process, we have many opportunities to grow and learn what not to do, because it doesn't feel right in our heart. We don't need people telling us how sinful we are, nor do we need to get caught up in pointing fingers at how sinful other people are. That behavior is toxic to the very essence of life. We need people to say how beautiful we are in the process. Love always wins.

Sin is *not* an action. Sin is a wrong belief about how we think God sees us. Which often comes from a distorted vision of who we think God is and who we are. What if, *all* of humanity has been born perfect and no one has ever fallen from Gods love, favor, and kindness?

Three

REPENTANCE AND BAPTISM

Have you ever heard you need to repent or get baptized be made right with God? We both have many times. Before we heard the message of "inclusion," we were taught repenting was asking God to pardon us for our actions, and baptizing was being dunked in water for remission of our bad behaviors. Afterwords, we needed to straighten up our lives, because God wasn't in the business of forgiving people over and over and over again. These ideas of repentance and baptism are cornerstones to many of the churches and denominations around the world. Their belief is those who turn to God in genuine repentance and faith will be saved, and others believe once baptized, the old life is gone and a new life awaits. These both go hand in hand in most religions around the world. The variations may be different, but the idea that we need to do something to please God or do something to be accepted by God is the same.

Sounds good, right? Repentance was taught to us as the changing of direction because of our sincere regret for some bad deed we have done or some dirty thought we have had. However, this change of direction, often considered repentance, seldom lasts for any length of time. The reason it doesn't have lasting results has to do with our deep ingrained misunderstanding of the too-good-to-be-true news that we were created out of love. This misunderstanding produces fear, doubt, and anxiety which cause us to continue struggling.

The *good news* is our efforts have *no* effect on God's favor and kindness to us. We can't stop it. His Love pours abundantly on *all* mankind.

"How foolish can you be? After starting your new lives in the Spirit, why are you now trying to become perfect by your own human effort?" (-Galatians 3:3 New Living Translation)

This teaching is driven by self-effort and selfishness. Francois Du Toit says, "A legalistic mind-set, the flesh, sponsors typical behavior that expresses itself in very visible symptoms."

If "repent" has anything to do with our works, it is in direct contradiction with the *too good to be true news* about our identity. The Greek word *metanoia*, which has been commonly translated as repent, does *not* mean us changing our actions or begging for God's love and favor. *Metanoia* means to change our mind about what we believe about the Father, Son, and Spirit.

In the book of Acts chapter 2, verse 38, after the Spirit of God came bellowing out of the Apostles, Peter said, "Repent, and let every one of you be baptized in the name of Jesus Christ for the remission of sins; and you shall receive the gift of the Holy Spirit." (-Acts 2:38)

This verse has great significance for *all* mankind. First, this was a Jewish individual who had grown up with 611 rules they had placed on themselves to attempt to please an already pleased God. This idea that God loved them unconditionally was totally new to the Jewish world, and much of the rest of the world as well. Peter had just had the assurance of God come out of his belly like rivers of living water.

The people around him and his friends at first thought they were all drunk, and it was early in the day. When Peter proclaimed "a God that is all love, who has no requirements to earn His love, The Spirit of Assurance flowed out of the entire audience. They all realized how perfectly and wonderfully they were made. This same thing happens when the *too good to be true news* is proclaimed today. Because, despite what religion and the world tells people, everyone is complete and perfect just the way they are. And neither death nor life will keep you from your intimate, everlasting relationship with your Creator.

Behavior, good or bad, will never change God's love for humanity! Believing this will produce peace and joy in our lives that will exceed anything we could ever dream. We are perfect, righteous, and holy! The relationship we have with our Creator needs no repentance. Repentance comes from the Latin Word *penance*, which means to pay for something. From this, the word repentance then means to repay for something that was already bought.

Whether you believe in Jesus or not, no one, including yourself or God, must buy you back into His favor and kindness. Jesus was not paying your debt; you don't need to pay a debt to God. Because there is no debt.

Jesus was ending a sacrificial system the Jewish population had created for themselves, His life, death, and resurrection are also a phenomenal reminders to the rest of the world that even death or bad behavior toward God will not separate any of us from His love.

Change your mind about who God is, and you will be immersed in assurance of the good news about your identity, which will set you free, and your life will become filled with peace and joy.

How does this happen?

Our Experience

Several years ago, we had the pleasure of meeting a man called Earl C at a Narcotics Anonymous convention on the West Coast.

This was a time in our lives when we both found hope through the 12-step model. We were traveling around to big conventions, listening to speakers tell where they came from and how their lives had changed. We were wandering around the convention hall and got to talking to this older gentleman. The softness of his eyes and wisdom of his face drew us in, intrigued by whatever nuggets of wisdom we may get from this encounter. The paper-thin skin of his arm caught our attention as he put out his hand to shake ours. The tattoo on his forearm seemed as aged as he was and very hard to make out. As we began to talk, he shared his testimony.

We were moved to our core once we heard about his "spiritual" experience. Still to this day, we recall how awesome it was to have him share with us his path. He didn't go into full detail about the murder he had committed. But he was an old-time addict who grew up in California, committed a heinous crime and had been sentenced to death. While on death row, his fate was approaching fast. He told us that when he ordered his last meal, he had zero hope, it was given a few moments before they were going to take him down to be executed. He told us how he collapsed on the floor in total shame and guilt. He cried out to God for the first time in his life, and he felt a comfort come over him. He knew that even though he was going to be executed in minutes that he was going to be OK. The guards prepped him, cuffed him, and he was waiting on the escort to lead him down to the hallway to his physical end, which he had peace about, not because he didn't commit an awful crime, but because he knew God loved him.

WHAT IF?

Hearing this sent chills down our arms, and we waited to hear what happened next. The idea of a God that loved us was new to us, so hearing this from someone in Narcotics Anonymous was something neither of us had really heard before. We were hanging on his every word. How could anyone have peace on the way to be executed? His eyes got brighter as he shared his experience, and the love was flowing out of him. He said he had cried out to God and then had peace in what his fate was going to be. Then the escort showed up and Earl was told the Governor had just pardoned him, which meant his life was spared. Over the next few years while in prison, he got to know God. He felt strongly that he needed to help troubled addicts get clean so they didn't end up where he had been. He had no understanding of why the Governor would pardon him.

A few years later he was paroled, but the state of California felt it was best if he wasn't released into their state. So they sent him to Seattle, Washington. When he arrived in Seattle, he found out that NA didn't have any meetings in the area, so he contacted NA and they rented a place for a meeting to happen. Earl showed up every day, made coffee, and waited for people to show up. During the first year no one else showed up, but Earl's passion to help others get clean and meet a loving God didn't waver. Eventually people showed up and the meeting got so big they would split them into more meetings, and this happened over and over. By the time we met him in 2007, the Seattle, Tacoma area had the largest group of members in the entire world. We became friends with Earl and for the next few years, we had multiple phone conversations. Earl passed away in 2010, and up until his death, he was committed to helping others find peace and experience life as a productive member of society.

Even though neither of us are currently active or involved in any of the Twelve-Step recovery programs, remembering this encounter with Earl and our relationship with him still gives us chills. We never knew his last name, we only knew him as Earl C. from Seattle. For years we didn't know the significance of how Earl got off of death row and was saved from execution minutes before he was going to be. But the last few years we realize the peace Earl found was the baptism of Assurance, and in this Assurance, God intervened. Earl had no assurance when he fell to the floor and prayed to God one final time before his execution. The assurance came from his core and he knew he was going to be OK. The Spirit of God lifted him up and he realized something greater than him unconditionally. As a result of this unwavering love, he was pardoned and eventually placed back into society to give people hope, bless them with love, and show them that things happen in our lives that can never be explained and can never be denied. His gift of life was a shock. It didn't make any sense, because he was guilty. Earl did not tell us he confessed all his dirty doing's or repented. What he said was he cried out to God in desperation and God met him with love.

Earl's example is just one of many that could be shared. in fact, if all of us took time to think, we all probably have one or two moments in our lives where these type of situations have happened, when peace has come bubbling out of us when things looked like gloom. This example is a very real example that assurance has nothing to do with what we do or don't do and everything to do with how loved we are from our creator. It is not about us believing in Jesus but about God's belief in us.

What if, God's love for us does not require repentance or baptism?

Four

CONFESSION

Just like "repentance," the "confession of our sins'" become a cornerstone in many churches and denominations around the world. Even though the word confess is only used in three verses in the entire New Testament.

Is it possible that the modern Christian church has made it way more important than the early church? Why has the importance of *confession* increased over time? Both of these questions came to the surface for us the longer we were on the Grace Road. We discovered the meaning of the word is completely out of context. In most Christian contexts the word confess or confession is being honest about some troublesome action we have done or some thought we have had. However, the word that has been translated as confession is *homologeo*, which means "to speak what God says about who we are." What a difference in the meaning. The misleading teachings about this word have been a way many churches (denominations) keep the money flowing in and their attendance high. We believe the real issue is this idea of confessing our "bad stuff " has caused many people to struggle with unworthiness, shame, guilt, and fear of eternal punishment. We don't believe in the confession that is taught in church, which is to confess all the wrong things we have done to God, so he can

48

then absolve us from his punishment that we would receive if we didn't confess.

We believe when we confess what God says about us this will produce success in every area of our lives. This is true confession. True confession is proclaiming the truth about your identity, that is *you are loved and perfect just the way you are.* Proclaiming these simple truths will cause everything in your life to flourish. The good news is *everyone* is His perfect masterpiece. Designed perfectly, created for excellence, and destined to live in peace and joy. You are loved and have enormous value.

Katy's Experience

When I was in treatment at the Meadows in Wickenburg, Arizona, I had a spiritual awaking. This part of my journey started me on a path of self-acceptance and love. When I walked into the meeting room for the first time, there was a partition dividing the larger room into two smaller rooms. About halfway through the room there was a circle of chairs, probably ten to twelve seats, which sat sterile, cold, and waiting to be filled with the evening group of patients that decided to attend the nightly AA meeting. Every night we had to choose what 12-step meeting we would attend. We could choose between Codependency Anonymous (CODA), Narcotics Anonymous (NA), Alcoholics Anonymous (AA), Depression Anonymous, Sexual Addictions Anonymous (SA), or Gamblers Anonymous (GA). The meeting I chose to go to was AA. In a room full of 10-12 people, we went around and introduced ourselves. When it was my time to speak, I remember saying, "I am an alcoholic and my name is Katy." It had been my daily routine for the previous six years leading up to my stay at the Meadows. I never thought anything of it. Why would I have? I had been attending one to three meetings a day for six years and it had become my routine and belief about myself. However, there are two things that I will never forget about this day.

The first thing I learned was how easy it is to get looked up to as if you have life figured out just because you are sober. I had that epiphany when, after we said our names, we also announced our sobriety time. Another gentlemen and I had years of "sobriety" The gentleman had twelve years, and I was coming up on six years of complete sobriety from drugs and alcohol. After we both identified ourselves, the room got still and everyone who spoke that night looked up to us like we were some gurus who had it figured out. I remember thinking, and at the end of the meeting sharing, that we may have long term sobriety, but we were both at the Meadows because of suicidal thoughts and massive depression. Sobriety doesn't mean anything if there isn't a quality of life that follows.

An even more life changing lesson came from this encounter. I had just identified myself by saying, "I am an alcoholic and my name is Katy." Inflated by some ego and lots of fear, I put off a false sense of security with my sobriety, but I so desperately wanted to stop the feelings of insecurity, unworthiness, and hopelessness. I could say with all the confidence in the world that I was an alcoholic and my name was Katy. That was the ego of thinking I had won some grand champion ribbon because I could put days together sober. I remember feeling full of shame every time I spoke though, because I had put together sobriety, but I was dying inside. I desired peace. I desired connection. I desired a community of people that did more with their lives than put together days of sobriety and live in meetings. I wished at the time I could have articulated what I was feeling. Instead a gentleman interrupted me and asked if I would repeat what I said, so I did: "I am an alcoholic and my name is Katy." I said it again but honestly, I was irritated that he was interrupting me. "I am sorry could you repeat that again," he said, this time asking me to pay attention to what I was saying. Again I said, "I am an alcoholic and my name is Katy." Interrupting a third time he said, "Do you hear what you are saying?" I was thinking, "You fucking idiot, I know exactly what I am saying." Irrational at this point, feeling very disrespected and almost bullied I said, "What do you mean?" His response changed everything for me that day and opened my eyes to a spiritual truth I had been blinded to until this moment. He looked at me with the most compassionate eyes. He was a Buddhist by orientation and told me the following "You are Katy first." He said it again, "You are Katy first." Every time you have spoken you have spoken your problem as your identity and then gave your name like some insignificant closing to a real sad story, but you are Katy first. Don't ever forget you are a person who has a lot more than an ailment to identify yourself as. His wisdom overwhelmed me and reality hit my heart so heavily that I was not sure what to do with myself, because the false identity of who I was was killing my chances of ever becoming who I was created to be. I often think about that moment, blessed and overwhelmed that someone who didn't know me at all shared that spiritual truth with me. Those words were like dynamite to a rocky foundation of existence I had been living in and have since given me a voice that, over time and understanding, I can see is bold, beautiful, and loved.

"The entire cosmos is the object of God's affection! And he is not about to abandon his creation-the gift of his son is for humanity to realize their origin in him who mirrors their authentic birth-begotten not of flesh but of the Father! In this persuasion the life of the ages echoes within the individual and announces that the days of regret and sense of lostness are over!"
(-John 3:16 Mirror Bible)

It is so clear now, after having the revelation's that all of creation is intertwined with God and the rest of creation. Living with the understanding that we are perfect just the way we are has allowed us to confess the reality of our being. Knowing that we are fully immersed in connection with the Creator of the world inspires us to live rather than be paralyzed by fears and distractions of the false beliefs we have about ourselves.

How refreshing the truth is, when interpreted properly, the verse completely lines up with dozens of other verses that tell us we are in right standing with God. This is the Good News that expands the eye of the storms we live in. We are His and He is ours!

51

WHAT IF?

The world tells us to get right with our soul, that confession is a key component. In many cases, it helps. However, reminding ourselves how wonderfully we were made, rather than our screw ups, will ultimately change our life. The good news is we are whole and complete the moment we are given breath. We never needed forgiveness, so we don't have to ask or beg to be healed and forgiven. We don't have to tell God about what we believe we have done wrong to be forgiven, because God isn't upset with us. Therefore, there is nothing for which we need to be forgiven.

Again, true confession, life-changing confession, is agreeing with God that we are perfect, righteous, and holy.... Claiming who we really are! Proclaim who you truly are on a regular basis and watch your world change before your very eyes. Living in the freedom you have in your identity is key to living in peace and joy.

Five

YOUR CREATOR

The area we live in is a predominantly Christian region. Seventeen miles from where we live is a Ten Commandment park with a visitor center. What we saw displayed and used to believe is Jesus loved us, but God hated who we were, because we did not fit the model of the church. In order for Him to look at us, we needed to go through some ritual so He could see us through the blood of Jesus. This concept of God causes many struggles with security and our identity. If we believe in a God that doesn't really like us, it is difficult for us to have any security in our heart. If God *"is the same today, tomorrow and yesterday."* (-Hebrews 13:8 NKJV), then is He the loving God that the Apostles Paul and John and Jesus said He is? Or is He the angry tyrant of Christianity's Old Testament, the Jews' Torah, and the Muslim's Quran? All three of these contain many of the same stories of an angry, jealous, punishing God, who has a thirst for blood.

From our experiences, as well as the peace we get in our hearts when we read about the God that Jesus, Paul and John described, we believe that this same loving God can be found all over the world. We are able to see Him in people's faces and actions everywhere we go He is alive and well. Also, we understand that Christians don't have the only ticket for people to find their true identity in Love. In many of the teachings and beliefs around the world, His Love shines through. While our influence and experience with a loving God has happened when we reexamined our faith, we are thrilled to tell you that God is Love and God is everywhere we look.

The heart checks we have had on this journey on the Grace Road continue to grow outside the confines of Christianity. Because Spiritual truths are spiritual truths. While having these heart checks has opened our eyes and our ears to a totally new and, some would say, radical view of who are Creator is, we realize our vision of God is growing daily. Today we see the Creator as many things, including our Father, our Mother, and our Husband. We believe everyone was created in their image and likeliness to be in healthy loving relationship with them. We don't believe we were created to be servants to God the Father, Jesus, or the Holy Spirit. We weren't born to their worshipers, or for them to harass us.

To understand this, we had to take a hard look at what the personality is of our Creator, and what we found has impacted our entire existence.

Kurt's Experience

I grew up attending church periodically as a youth and fairly often as a teenager but seldom as an adult before Katy was miraculously healed in 2011. In October 1998, as I was backing up my car from the apartment complex I was living in to go to work, my vehicle struck an older man I had known for years. He was the father of one of my close friends from the previous decade. Immediately, I went into shock. At first, the medics on the scene thought he would be fine; he had hit his head on the concrete, but the impact didn't seem drastic. Within hours he was in a coma and passed away a few days later. My whole life got smothered in guilt and shame.

Law enforcement took me to the police station for routine questioning and alcohol testing. I was alone. Fortunately, my four-year-old son was at his mom's. I felt the world cave in on me as if a darkness came in around me. This began to smother me, and as a result I collapsed on my kitchen floor that evening and wept, screamed, and cried for hours. At the time I didn't know what the outcome was going to be. Within the week, I heard statements like "God only gives you what you can handle." Each time I heard it I nearly puked. If God had anything to do with this, I wanted nothing to do with Him or Her, or whatever God was.

The belief that this loving God would cause this to happen infuriated me. Then the idea that God didn't like me began to creep in. The months started to go by, and even though the legal system found me innocent from any fault for his death, I could not shake the guilt and shame. Well-meaning Christian's continued to put their spin on the accident. I heard things like "This is a test from God for you to get closer to Him." My thought when I heard this was always, "You have to be kidding? Who in their right mind would want to get close to a bi-polar, psycho, controlling God who plays games like that?"

As time passed, I began to attempt to mask the shame and guilt with drugs, more drugs, sex, self-loathing, gambling and debating every Christian who would engage with me. The blackness had fully crept in, and I was pitiful. When at the casino, I would not play any number that had a seven in it or could be divide by seven, because I saw the number of seven as the number of God. In my mind, God and I were not on the same team, so I was not going to have any part of that God. This may seem odd, but it was where I was. I got physically and mentally ill when I thought about the God the Christians had told me about. I came to a crossroads in my life. I knew I couldn't keep using drugs and sex the way I was. I no longer was able to run from the guilt, shame, and darkness that had been smothering me for years. I made the decision I needed to take my life, but in order for it to seem like an accident, I knew I needed to clear my head. Because I knew people who had gotten clean in Narcotics Anonymous, I asked my friend Jim, who was involved in recovery, if he would take me to a meeting. My plan was to get clean, get a clear head, and make a solid plan to take my life. In desperation I ended up in Narcotics Anonymous in January of 2005.

I got clean off drugs, quit going to the casino, and quit using sex to attempt to escape. As I looked around the room, I realized some of the people seemed to be happy and have freedom. So I decided to give life one more chance. But the self-loathing and anger at God didn't subside. Thanks to my persistence and desire to be considered one of the over-comers, I continued on the journey of life. After a year of sobriety, I was at a birthday celebration for all the people who had reached a milestone. I was told by an individual that unless I accepted Jesus as my savior, "I would not make it another year." Sadly, the individual who told me that passed away a few months later, and at the time I was pissed because I was going to prove him wrong because that God and Jesus that he loved so much were not people I wanted anything to do with. The years in recovery came and went, but the guilt, shame, and anger stayed close. Any time something bad happened, I thought once again that God was punishing or testing me, and I wanted nothing to do with it.

After Katy ended up in a treatment center, the bills in our life began to pile up. Her medication alone was around twenty-five hundred dollars a month, and much of the time between when our vehicle went off the cliff and she was healed, she couldn't work. This led us to joining a network marketing company with the hopes and dreams of creating enough income to not continue to drown. I knew if we were going to make any money, I would have to get connected with someone who was making money.

I was put in contact with Ron Yeager, who lives in Colorado Springs. During our first phone conversation, he asked me what church I attended. And as politely as I could, because I knew I needed his help to make cash, I said something to the effect of "I know a lot of you guys go to church and that is great for you, but I didn't get involved to get saved. I got involved with this company to make money." Ron got quiet but said, "Thanks for being honest."

Over the next few years, Ron and I talked on the phone almost daily, at first only about the business of making money, but eventually about how to treat other people, including Katy. Ron became the first Christian in my adult life who didn't seem to be friends with me only to save me.

This made me think, "Did I miss something in this Christian thing?" So, I asked Katy if she wanted to go to church with me. She had been attending here and there, but now I was willing to go. Ron had softened me up enough that when she would go to church, I didn't judge or debate her. But until I asked her to attend together, I wasn't sure I wanted to get face to face with God again. But Ron's God that shined through him seemed different.

Katy and I started attending a church that seemed far removed from the church and Christians I knew. The environment of the church was young, hip and what at the time seemed more relevant to my life than a stale cold building. When worship would begin, the lights would go out, strobe lights would come on and people would act almost like they were at a concert than church. The pastor was young, energetic and had a speaking style that could hold my focus. He would not only talk about the Bible but he always had a way of intertwining self-help and personal development into his sermons. As out of the ordinary as it was for church culture, it was the environment I needed to begin to look at God and Christianity through a different lens. We joined a small group, but nothing was changing. The God I was hearing about was that same angry judgmental God who only liked some, hated others, and couldn't look at any of us unless we believed in the son that was beaten and tortured on our behalf for all the bad stuff we had done. Still, I was desperate, so I kept going. I often got frustrated with the small group leaders, the pastor, and everything about the church. But I didn't think we had anywhere else to go, and Katy was seeming to enjoy the messages and the fellowship.

Earlier in the book, I shared about the tree I had seen in the parking lot. This was the moment I was baptized in the assurance that I am loved, have always been loved, and forever will be loved. The Spirit living deep in my heart came out like rivers of living water filling every crevice of my body. I was healed in that parking lot from over a decade of severe shame, guilt, suicidal thoughts, and I was set free from the darkness that at times had suffocated completely paralyzed me. I felt like a new person. My heart was jumping for joy. The gospel had come alive in me.

When Katy and I got back to Kalispell, we went to dinner and had one of the biggest arguments we have ever had. I told her that I thought we should start something in Kalispell connected to Ron and Marthie's church in Colorado, and because Katy was finally feeling like she found some where she belonged our conversation became an argument.

So I asked a friend, Nathan, who was part of the small group we were a part of in Kalispell, to coffee. I told him what I thought we should do, and that since I was the head of the household I believed she should follow, but how could I make her? I didn't really believe this "Christian" stuff about me lording over her. But I thought that if I was in this Christian practice, I would use it in this case, because I really thought this was best. In my heart, I realized this example of bullying my way with scripture wasn't good. I believe man and woman are equals. They each have a say, and each one's opinions and feeling are just as valuable as the others.

Nathan didn't give me an inch: "It is great that you're the head of the household, but being the head means putting others first. And men are told to put the woman first. So, if Katy feels like staying at the church she is going to, you have to keep going with her, and if you think messages from Freedom Ministries will fill you up, then you figure out how to listen to them on your own time." My bubble was burst. I thought for sure Nathan would encourage me and give me insight on how to get Katy to come along as we started something connected to the church in Colorado.

Everything stayed status quo for a few months, Then Katy and I ended up in Portland, Oregon when Mike and Barb Popovich were there. Ron had told them we were in the same area as them, so Mike called us and asked us if we wanted to join them for dinner in their hotel suite.

When we walked in, the two of us were nearly dropped to our knees. Something had filled the room. Love was overpowering. After a brief conversation and at the start of dinner, Mike leaned over and told me that he was willing to help me start the fellowship in Kalispell that I had felt moved to get going. Katy at first thought I had talked to him about it ahead of time. But when it became clear that, other than Nathan, I hadn't talked to anyone about it, she warmed up to the idea. A few months later in December of 2011, we started a house fellowship that has continued since.

Over the course of the next few years, the belief about who God really is has continued to bellow out of my heart, and what started as the washing away of guilt and shame has continued to grow. God loves me and accepts me for who I am. He didn't orchestrate the accident. He wasn't testing or punishing me.

Last summer I heard the author of The Shack, Wm Paul Young, say something so profound and totally new to me that more of the unraveling of my wrong beliefs about who God is came off with a vengeance. "God is the Creator of Life. God is not the author of Life." This simple statement is how I view God today. He knows my beginning and my end. I am not talking about the day I physically die. God knew me from the foundation of the world. He gave me the gift of life in this world that I get to experience and the eternal paradise everyone gets to enjoy when their soul leaves this earthly body.

It is wild to think about the ride my life has been and continues to be. My creator loves everyone! It's not contingent on what we believe or don't believe. Because He is in and through everything and everyone. When I look back on my darkest hour, it is amazing that I had people in my life who were and still are the mirror image of God. I was surrounded by people of his likeness and image: Katy, Ron and Marthie, our son Zac, my brother Greg and his wife Lori, my mom and my dad Bob, my dad Fred, my brother Brad and many others. Even though I was blind to it because of my own self-pity and loathing, they each attempted to lift me up and did not judge me. They were at times the mirror image of who God really is. Even though it took the miraculous for me to see who God really is, now, years later, I see him in the faces I meet, and I am moved to share the love of God with everyone I meet. When they don't hear or want to hear about a God that loves everyone, I don't get discouraged because His Spirit resides in me and everyone I meet. Sometimes it just takes the baptism of assurance at the right time to hear it. The truth is everyone is God's masterpiece and He is never disappointed with us.

One of the greatest revelations we have had is knowing who the Holy Spirit is, what her function is and understanding that she has the same character and personality as God the Father and our Husband Jesus Christ. The Holy Spirit is often referenced in female pronoun in the Hebrew, Aramaic, and Greek language from which the Bible has been translated. The reason is because She is the perfect mother, the mother we have always wanted to have in our life. She is our friend. She is our encourager. She will lift us up when we fall and scrape our knee. She will clean up the wounds we have in life with love and affection. She comforts us when things don't seem to be going well. She, along with our Father and our Husband, will always love us, protect us, and help us.

When She reminds us, she doesn't convict us of some crime. She reminds us of who we really are, who we have always been, and how we are destined for great things. She reassures us *"in love, joy, peace, endurance, kindness, goodness, faith, and gentleness"* (*-Galatians 5:22 NLT*)

We were all born of Her. She is the mother of everyone who has breath and, just like our Father and our Husband, she will never leave us.

60

What if the Father is who Jesus and the Apostles John and Paul said He is? John is the only one of the original twelve apostles who died of old age and not a martyr's death. Most theologians believe he was the youngest of the Apostles, yet Jesus put much trust in him when he asked him to care for his earthly mother when he was nearing death on the cross.

John didn't learn to write until his later years, and he is believed to be the author of five books that are included in most Bible versions: Gospel of John, the epistles 1John, 2John, 3John, and the Book of Revelation. Many theologians believe one of his students, Poly Carp, encouraged him to write the Gospel of John and the Book of Revelation to share what he personally saw as an eye-witness and companion of Jesus Christ. Some experts believe Matthew and John wrote their own Gospels. Matthew was the tax collector Jesus met during the last three years of his earthly existence. Mark was written by a companion of Peter, and Luke was a doctor who is said to have known Paul, Peter, and John and is also the author of the Book of Acts. At least three other Gospel stories were written during the first few decades following Jesus's death, dissension into Hades, resurrection from Hades, and ascension to Paradise. These books have been translated in the last century and are the Gospel of Peter, the Gospel of Thomas, and the Gospel of Mary Magdalene.

These Gospels written by Peter, Thomas, and Mary Magdalene are not included in the Cannon (Bible).

After his time with Jesus, John spent the rest of his life proclaiming the good news to the masses, and his credentials are without flaw. John described God as love. *"To not [know] love is to not know God. Love is who God is." (-1John 4:8 Mirror Bible)*

John also tells us that Jesus said, "If you have seen me then you have seen the Father, because we are the same" *(See John 14:9).*

This means the character of Jesus is the same as the Father. And the character of Jesus was to love and help everyone with whom he came into contact to remind the self-righteous rock throwers that he saw the ones they deemed as dirty and needed to be stoned to death as clean perfect brides and children *(See John 8:1-11)*.

John also wrote that Jesus said the Father judges no one *(See John 5:22-23)*. And that he also judges no one *(See John 12:47-48)*. John also believed the Holy Spirit was his friend, advocate, mother, and guardian because he recounted Jesus telling him and others that they would live their entire life with the Her, just as he had *(See John 14:17)*.

The Apostle Paul's gospel (too-good-to-be-true) story was written in the Book of Acts. In this Book, Luke tells the story of Stephen *(See Acts 7)*, where Saul, whom after his encounter with the Lord went by Paul, witnessed and participated in the stoning of Stephen, who believed the Creator of *all* also loved *all*. Then as Saul was traveling around the region rounding up anyone who believed God was love, he was charged and found guilty of this belief and the belief that Jesus had ended the sacrificial system the Jewish nation practiced. When they were found guilty, they would be put to death for this belief. When Paul met the Lord on the Road to Damascus (See Acts 9), God appears and asks Paul, "Why are you persecuting me?" Paul fell to his knees and asked him, "Who are you?" God responds, "I am Jesus. Now get up and go to the city of Damascus and you will be told what to do." For three days Paul was in compete darkness; his eyes were open but day and night he was unable to see. Then Ananias, who believed God was love, went to Paul and laid hands on him, and the Love that was deeply buried in Paul's heart behind all the rules, laws, fear, and hate came to the surface and he was able to see the world and God's entire creation for the first time.

Paul went on to write many letters to people who were for the first time beginning to see that God was love, and he had loved them all from the foundation of the world. His letters make up nearly two thirds of the New Testament. And just like us, his understanding of who God really is grew over time, and He had to correct things he had previous thought, which is clear in 2 Corinthians, in which he was correcting some of his thoughts he had written in 1 Corinthians. Paul wrote that we are not born out of Spirit of Fear, but out of Spirit of a sound mind to clear up the idea we are to fear God. We are wonderfully made, not "fearfully" and wonderfully made. Paul also wrote to both non-Jewish populations and Jewish populations.

Years ago, we heard a few messages on "rightfully dividing the Bible," which explained how in the New Testament we need to understand who it was written to how it pertains to us. We learned that nine epistles were written to people who were not Jewish and had not put themselves under a law to attempt to please a God they didn't know. This cleared up a lot of confusion, and we spent countless hours learning what Paul wrote to people who were not Jewish in Romans, 1Corinthians, 2Corinthians, Galatians, Ephesians, Philippians, Colossians, 1Thessalonians, and 2Thessalonians.

What we found was the clear truth, that the Father of all of mankind loves everyone. And Nothing can or ever will separate us from His unwavering love.

"The entire cosmos is the object of God's affection! He is not about to abandon his creation the gift of his son is for humanity to realize their origin in him who mirrors their authentic birth-be-gotten not of flesh but of the Father! In this persuasion the life of the ages echoes within the individual and announces that the days of regret and sense of being lost are over! God has no intention to condemn anyone he sent his son, not to be the Judge but the Savior of the world." (-John 3:16-17 Mirror Bible)

WHAT IF?

The freedom we found in the Gospel changed our beliefs and in some cases caused others to distance themselves from us. Many people we were associated with felt like with us sharing our revelation and experience that we were leading people away from God, we even had a experience at our local fellowship where a person attending yelled at us that we were leading people to hell. But the good news we found produced freedom like we had never experienced before. Just like Paul, we all have personal experiences with veils of wrong-beliefs that have kept us in the dark. But when we realized that the Creator of *all* is not a tyrant, many veils came off of our eyes.

The Spirit, the Father of Creation, and your Husband are all love. They keep no records of wrongs and will love you forever. The good news is this is not based on your belief in Jesus or your unbelief. For us, we found the love of all Creation in our study and in the understanding of who the Trinity really are and how they feel about us. We realize this was because of who we met in a time of crisis in our life. They met us with love and compassion. Because of their belief in Jesus, we searched this message of Love to find who God is to us. We have been greatly impacted by what we see as the Spirit and the Father. But we also know that the Creator of *all* is not tied up in one belief system and can be found anywhere we look.

Because He, She, or They are in and through all things. And the Spirit of Truth and Life resides in everyone and She jumps in excitement when we see ourselves the way the Creator has seen us all along. What if the trinity really is in all of hwnanity?

Six

THE ENEMY

The Apostle John wrote about his eye-witness account where Jesus was talking to a small group and said, *"The enemy's purpose is to steal, kill, and destroy" (See John 10:10).* Who is the enemy, Jesus was talking about? Some theologians believe Jesus was talking about the teachers of the Mosaic Law, who taught a ritual system to earn God's favor and blessing. While others believe it is Satan. The answer to this question lies in Jesus's purpose to set the people free from the idea they are not good enough to be considered God's children.

For years we worked hard, followed programs and worked the twelve steps searching for freedom, peace and joy. We spent money and we looked to the medical community for divine health, and we ended up broke and sick. Our story isn't unique. Most people have had times where peace and joy seemed unattainable. Like many others, we felt like we were living in hell. We screamed about the situations we were in and worked harder to please a "God" we knew nothing about and had no idea about His character. We were frozen in fear, so overwhelmed by doing the wrong thing we couldn't move. We wept with guilt behind closed doors and we hid in shame trying to cover up that feeling with a false sense of pride and inflated ego.

WHAT IF?

Even in this darkness of not knowing who we were or how valuable we are to God, we saw the Light and met the Light face to face. We have shared some of the miracles we saw, but we also saw many people who had been healed fall back into the same illness months later. We pressed in harder and harder in desperation to heal the sick and reach the lost. But the harder we worked the less we saw, and the more tired we became. In our hearts we knew something was missing and early on we knew it had something to do with *"guarding our hearts with all diligence, for out of the heart springs the issues of our life" (See Proverbs 4:23)*. We didn't know what that meant and went down many rabbit holes in our quest to find the answer.

Today we have a much better understanding about the value of guarding our hearts from lies that claim we are anything other than perfect. We also see the importance of sowing the truths about who we really are into our soul. God is love; love is what we are. The voice of the Spirit echoes in our hearts when we hear how wonderfully we are made, how we are all destined for great things, for perfect health, and it cringes when we hear the lies of the enemy.

Who is the enemy? The enemy is any idea or teaching that anyone is born a dirty misbehavior or that we grow into having a misbehaving nature.

God loves everyone. In all four of the Gospels, the stories that are in the Bible, they shared how Jesus served communion to Judas even though he knew he was going to betray him. The truth is Judas is completely loved by The Creator of the world and is undoubtedly in paradise with him today

The enemy, often referred to as Satan has been portrayed as many things -from a demon with horns to a beautiful manipulator.

But the enemy is not a person or a spirit. The enemy is any teaching that promotes hate, fear, or exclusiveness. Whether it's religious-based or not, anything that doesn't give assurance of our perfection to *all* mankind is the enemy.

Guilt, shame, and fear are the silent killers, and those feelings can cause us confusion and many times lose decades of our lives. Those feelings also cause health, financial, and relationship problems. Nothing opposes the too-good-to-be-true-news more than they do. They, the enemy, will tell us all that God is angry at us and that we need to do something to please him. They may tell us that we are not good enough and don't deserve good things, because God doesn't want us to prosper. These distorted ideas about who we are and who God is, breaks up families, destroy careers, and squash dreams, because they cause judgement. They are the enemy and will flee when the good news about who we truly are is shared.

Overcoming the darkness of the enemy is foundational in what the life we live looks like.

Our Experience

A few years ago, we were asked to come to Kalispell Regional Hospital to pray for a lady who was on life support. The doctors were having family say their goodbyes before they were going to take her off life support. Becky at the time was around thirty years old, a mother of two young kids. We don't know the details of why she was there, but she had a heart infection. The doctors and nurses gave her zero percent chance of living. When we showed up, we met our friend Nathan, a relative of Beckys husband. Nathan asked her dad if we could see her before everyone else to pray for her. He agreed, and after another few family members came out of the room, the three of us were let into ICU and went to her room. Her husband was in there, and we talked briefly. And then we started to pray. We told Becky how much God loved her, and we had maybe a five-minute conversation with God, thanked him for his supernatural touch on Becky. Thanked Him in advance for her miraculous healing.

After we left the ICU we went by a room, and Katy was moved to go into the room, and Nathan and I followed. A woman around seventy lay on a bed. She seemed unconscious, so Nathan left the room to go ask someone at the nurses' station what was going on with her health. During that time she came to, and she made direct eye contact with me. We had a conversation about how much God loved her. She told me she was afraid to see her sister again, and we told her she had nothing to worry about. She explained how guilty she felt. We reminded her that God keeps no record of wrongs, and when she is ready, she will get to embrace her sister again because she will be in Paradise with God and her sister. She lit up, her eyes sparkled for a few moments, and the darkness that covered her totally disappeared. She seemed to have total peace and joy, and then within seconds she went unconscious again.

When Nathan got back, he told us that the nurses said that she was nearing her end and there was nothing they could do, so they just hoped the transition from life was easy on her. The three of us left. We all thought, "It's so Good that God knows her."

The next morning Nathan called us. He had just been up to the hospital. It was obvious by the tone of his voice that he was thrilled to tell us something. He didn't mince words with idle chit chat. He immediately told us that Becky was completely better. The doctors didn't understand it, but she would be released the next day after another night of observation. He also told us that when he went by the older lady's room, it was empty. So, he went to the nurses' desk and asked if she had passed away. The nurse was in awe and told him that she had a miraculous turnaround, so the hospital released her that morning.

We were blown away. The shame and guilt she felt about what ever riff she had with her sister, and the doubt she had that God loved her nearly took her life. Yet, when she heard that God loved her unconditionally and that she would get to embrace her sister again when she was ready, everything changed.

Within a few hours we saw two people on death's door come back to life, despite what the medical community believed. The common denominator wasn't confession, repentance, or baptism. The thing they both needed to hear was they were loved by the one who created them.

Knowing we are loved is the way to living life in the freedom of assurance. It doesn't matter what your ethnicity is, your blood line, your political affiliation, your sexual orientation, or your religious affiliation or what you think you have done wrong. You are loved!

For us, this belief has radically changed our lives. We have begun to see others the way God sees them and, as a result, we have been able to see the way God sees us. Love, joy, and peace are evident when we guard our hearts against the lies we believe about who we truly are. This deep change in our hearts has brought us back to who we have been from the foundation of the world, meaning that *all* of human- ity has been loved by God from the beginning. God loves us without exception. Live overwhelmed by God's opinion of you! (See Philippines 4:7)

Let no fear distract you from who you are and how wonderfully you were created. You weren't born out of brokenness; you came from the love of God to commune with Him or Her. You were designed and created to live and enjoy life. You were not created to worship, praise, or attempt to earn God's love.

For us, meditating or visualizing what we want our life to be is what our life is becoming. We focus and thank God for the divine health we have. We focus and thank God for the supernatural financial increase in our life. We visualize what our lives will look like and how it makes us feel. In the last few years, the more we water our soul with the Good News, the easier it is to see the changes in our lives as if it is already complete.

Individually, we have truths that we need to focus on when we get angst in our gut about dreams we have. No dream or goal we have is impossible. If we get angst around the possibility of a goal or dream it is because of some lie we had previous been told about ourselves not being invincible. Those feelings of angst are not our fault and not ours to own.

Whether you desire divine health, supernatural finances, or perfect relationships, take the time to visualize what it looks like. A few years ago, we heard a story about a lady who was riddled with cancer. She put pictures all over her house of what she looked like when she was healthy and happy. She spent time every day remembering what it was like for her body to feel healthy. Over the course of a few months the cancer miraculously disappeared, and she was filled with peace and joy. By visualizing yourself the way God sees you and continuing to picture yourself that way amazing life changing transformations can and will happen. Our minds are powerful. Because your belief is your destiny.

What if everyone is perfectly and wonderfully made?

Seven

HELL

As we began to understand that God is love, the next logical step we took was to look at Hell. We know this is a "hot topic" in the Christian community today, and our take is not always received with open arms. The country is so divided. There are certain evangelists and pastors saying things like "Let the reality of Hell motivate you to speak to others about Heaven."

We have studied it for the last few years. Through that process we have come to understand Love always wins, and love keeps no record of wrongs! As we have mentioned before, Love is the character of God, which means Love is God. God is Love. Simple, but in many ways it is the most important message we have ever heard.

Kurts Experience

The first time I really grasped any idea that I was being taught about eternal Hell was when my Grandpa Jim passed away. To my brothers and me, our Grandpa was awesome. He played baseball with us, told us funny jokes, and made all sorts of fart noises with his hands and armpits. I was eleven when he passed away. After he passed away, I heard some adults saying that he was a great guy but was in Hell forever because he didn't openly profess his belief in Jesus. It shook me back then, and it continued to shake me for years

71

to come. This seemed to be the first time I caught what they meant when they talked about hell at church. Looking back, this was the first thing ever that I began to question, because it never felt right in my heart. As a result of this lie, I hung around church until I was nineteen, even though events and life's situations began piling up. At the heart of it all for me was how could a loving Creator, who created everyone and knew what our outcomes were going to be, get a kick out of torturing at least two thirds of his creation for all of eternity? Common sense was beginning to win in my heart.

I could not love a God who I thought may be sending me to a torturing furnace forever. I doubted anyone really loved God. I would hear well-meaning Christians say, "I would rather be right about Jesus than wrong when I die." Today I see that comment as a total fear response. God and Jesus are love, love never fails, and this love certainly is not contingent on what we do or say.

The idea that we need to fear God is the foundation of all teachings of hell. The concept of hell is a fairly new idea; it was not in the early church. None of the Apostles taught or believed in the hell that is currently being taught in church today. This teaching of hell was planted as seeds by St. Augustine and St. Jerome around 500 A.D with the concept of purgatory which was not a belief the early church held.

For nearly 1,000 years it stayed in the purgatory state, and then John Calvin took it to the modern fire and torture chamber that is still being taught. Calvin's influence also got the Catholic Church to add hell along with purgatory to their foundational after-life teachings. This twisted view of God and eternal life eventually reached all of Western Christianity. The Muslim faith also teaches hell in a very similar way.

Also, the concept "I need to fear the Lord and love Him with all my heart" does not make sense. We have talked in depth about this for years. When we have asked others about why we need to "fear the Lord," we have been told, "It really means to revere the Lord." Immediately when we hear this, we think, "Then why doesn't the Bible say that?" Why do we say you must "fear the Lord" rather than "revere the Lord"? When I have asked other believers in Jesus I was told, "Well, you're a believer so you revere God, but non-believers need to fear God."

During our quest to uncover the Good News in the idea we need to fear God, we learned this idea is listed at least twenty five times in the Old Testament. Fearing a vengeful, hateful God is the core of many of the stories. We learned that many people teach the idea that we need to believe in and revere God, but in order to revere him you must fear him first. They claim this is the rite of passage in order to make it to heaven.

Here lies the dilemma: "For God has not given us the spirit of fear; but a spirit of power, and of love, and of a sound mind" (2 Timothy 1:7). If God didn't give us a spirit of fear, then how could we be made fearful of God? What if we weren't fearfully and wonderfully made? What if we were just wonderfully made? It is clear that the Apostle Paul was attempting to correct this idea that people had in most religions around this time. Pagans were sacrificing virgins, Christians were sacrificing animals, in an attempt to keep a good relationship going with a blood-hungry God. But Paul was saying we should wait a minute because God is Love and Love keeps no record of wrongs. You don't need to sacrifice anything to Him, and you sure as heck have zero reason to fear Him!

God loves all of His creation!

When we looked up the word *revere*, we found that it means "to feel deep respect or admiration for something." When we looked up the definition for "fear," we found it is defined "as an unpleasant feeling triggered by the perception of danger."

The deeper we have gotten on the journey of meeting the God head, the more evident it has become that all three parts of the Trinity are Pure Love and we have zero reason to fear any of them. We don't have an unpleasant feeling triggered by a perception of danger. We have no reason to fear our Creator. We don't believe anyone else does either.

As we have already mentioned, Jesus told the teachers of the Law of Moses, the Pharisees that they didn't know the father. The Old Testament is not a direct reflection of God the Father or the Holy Spirit. There are glimpses where their true characters come out. However, in large this is not a book about who God really is.

It is easy to come to the conclusion that the idea we need to fear God isn't a bad translation from Hebrew to English but rather a distorted view of God by people who didn't know Him or His character.

It is good news when we realize we have no reason to fear our loving Father. It's then easy to rule out hell for those who don't come to believe or behave well before they die. We could break down all the times hell is translated from Greek in the New Testament, which is very few times. If you want that information, two great sources include the book *Hope Beyond Hell* by Gerald Beauchemin and part three of Don Keathley's *The Illusion of Hell* series that can be found on YouTube. Even though both sources affirmed us in what our heart was telling us, we believe theology doesn't outweigh what the word living in us tells us. And this is truly a heart issue.

Our hearts cannot reconcile with a God portrayed as happy or thrilled to torture and torment any of his creation. But our hearts jump for joy knowing that *all* get to experience paradise for all eternity!

We believe whole heartedly that *all* of creation will be embraced and celebrate together the undeniable love of the Creator upon their physical death. This is the Good News! Paradise is for the lost, for the broken, and for the proud...for every- one. When the time comes, all will be there; we will see Grandpa Jim again, and you will see everyone you have encountered in your life.

What if Everyone truly is the object of God's affection? Because God is love, there can be no eternal hell or darkness.

Eight

THE LAKE OF FIRE

This topic has been used by many to shame people and guilt people into believing that you need to be a Christian in order to be spared from eternal torture in the lake of fire. It never fully sat well in our hearts. The idea that our Creator, who created us in his likeliness and image, would stand before a fiery lake and toss all in who didn't conform seemed to us sick. In our world today, if someone was doing that to us in the flesh, they would be labeled a sociopath and be highly medicated and institutionalized. If it was a parent, Child Protective Services would remove the kids. Since we don't believe in eternal torture and torment, then you might be wondering about what the lake of fire talked about in Chapters nineteen and twenty in the Book of Revelations? What about where different translations suggest the deceivers (Satan and false prophets) and non-believers are thrown into the lake of fire, which is in the throne room of heaven where all of creation celebrating in praise by singing Holy, Holy is our God. This teaching doesn't sit well well in our hearts either. The Greek word used for holy is *agios* and in its purest definition means "others focused or others centered."

What this tells us is the angels and all the rest of creation are singing "others focused is our God." Others focused means

God is not a narcissist, his love is for *all* of humanity. He is not conditional. Our belief is everyone goes through a purification process, which is like a car wash that cleans our minds from any distorted-beliefs about who we are and who we have always been. This event is why everyone will be cheering when we get to Paradise! Because everyone is seeing themselves as the perfect masterpieces they truly are! Our Heavenly Father is so "others focused." Even if it takes physical death to see ourselves the way God has always seen us, it still will happen, despite ourselves. Salvation is your communion with God without your effort!

Katy's Experience

Last summer we were driving up to Whitefish, a small town about fifteen miles north of us in the mountains of Montana. Years ago, it had a quaint logging and railroad feel to it. Big Mountain is the ski resort nestled at the far end of the town, and the western corner of the town in hugged by Whitefish Lake. It is a beautiful town that, over the last fifteen years, has taken on a new identity of its own. Big Mountain, as the locals call it, is now named Whitefish Mountain, and the quaint town that was once filled with ski bums and railroad workers is now overtaken by big money and has a feel of Vail, Colorado.

While passing a small Baptist church on the crest of the hill before you drop into Whitefish, I noticed a sign outside: TOAST? or BREAD? IT'S YOUR ETERNITY... Instantly upon reading it my gut knotted up, followed directly by humor. I remember telling Kurt that if it is really a choice of toast or bread, I am all in on toast! Sadly in our society today we, take nonsense such as that sign or the other "fear" tactics that people use to manipulate us to set aside what our hearts are telling us and to agree with whatever sway people are trying to lead us into. Admittedly, there was a time in my life where I so wanted to please God by believing the rhetoric that was spoken, I started to think maybe people that I had loved and lost where spending eternity in hell. I am so glad that today my heart is boldly declaring how asinine that is. I do believe that we have times in our lives when situations are going on and the only way to describe them is hell. I have witnessed four close family friends experience the tragic loss of children, and during that time of anguish and torment, I think it would be a good assumption to describe that as hell. I have sat with friends who were going through horrific custody battles, and I would say that chapter of their lives as well as the kids' and the other parents' lives could be described as hell.

Several years ago, Kurt and I had a friend who really struggled with addiction. She liked anything that would make her escape the pain of her current reality. No matter how much love the people around her gave, she always resorted back to the needle, whether it be meth or heroine. In her early twenties, she contracted an infection in the valves of her heart. It is common for needle users to get this bacteria on their heart. If I remember correctly, it attached to the valves of her heart and was killing her. We were asked by the father of her children if we would go and see her at the hospital. Sara was on her death bed. She was told that if she didn't stop using drugs, she would die. Kurt and I loved Sara and we went to the hospital to see her. We walked down the hall at Kalispell Regional Hospital and upon getting to her room, there was an armed guard outside her door. We checked in at the nurse's station and went through the pat down process to visit her. I was taken back by the security. I knew she was sick but didn't think she had committed a crime, so the guard by the door didn't make any sense.

Upon entering, we were both devastated by the shape she was in. She was very thin, weak and worn out. We talked to her and made ourselves available for her any chance we could. When we left that day, we asked the nurses what the deal was with the security guard. They told us that people had previously smuggled Sara drugs while she was in the hospital and to protect her and keep her safe, they had to have the guard there.

Weeks went by and we visited frequently. Her heart got stronger, the infection seemed to heal up, and she was released. Over time we lost contact. Her response to texts or calls was less and less. A few months passed. We once again received a phone call, but this time it wasn't that Sara was in the hospital. She was on hospice and in order to get the care she needed she had to have a place to live. We allowed her to come stay with us. Kurt was just leaving for six weeks to work on the East Coast. She moved in the night before he left. When I saw her, I didn't fully understand why she was on hospice because hospice is for end of life comfort care only. She looked better than she had when we saw her a few months before. She had a nurse who would come and see her every other day and give her the medications she needed. Still to this day, I scratch my head when I think about all they gave her. She had Dilaudid and, Morphine for pain and Valium to help with anxiety. Sara was a needle-using drug addict. When the nurses would say, "Here are your meds, take them as prescribed" and leave them with her, I would scratch my head, thinking she had just given her a loaded gun and told her to play six rounds of Russian roulette.

Days went by and the addiction never settled down. During this process, I realized hell for a person struggling with addiction is wanting to quit, trying to quit, and being overtaken by the detox process, justifying starting using again. For two weeks this cycle went on. Spoons were disappearing from the silverware drawer. Light bulbs were disappearing from the cupboard as well as rooms that we barely used, I would come home and find her, and a few times another person, nodding out upstairs in her bedroom. The final straw happened just after a hellacious few days of holding her while she vomited, cleaning up because she was so sick she couldn't make it to the bathroom, and holding her through the gut-wrenching screams because her body and bones hurt so bad. I told her I couldn't do it anymore after the intense time I had just spent with her detoxing only to see her use again. She had to leave. In my mind, I would have walked hand and hand with her through the dying process if it was natural, but her continued use of drugs was too much for me to take. Kurt had now been gone three or four weeks. All I could do was share with him over the phone the insanity of the experience. I told her she had to leave.

I remember taking her to another one of her friend's house and dropping her off. A week had gone by and she asked if she could come back. I told her if she could honestly give up the drugs, she could. I picked her up and brought her back to our house. When we got inside, she handed me a makeup bag. I opened it up and there were about fifteen to twenty loaded up syringes. She asked me to get rid of them. I called her hospice nurse and she got admitted to the hospice wing at Kalispell Regional Hospital. I would say the ups and downs of her addiction felt like "hell."

After a few days in the hospital, Sara began to settle in. My mom brought her a pair of satin pajamas beautiful purple, so soft and gentle on her skin. She was dying and her body was failing fast. The joy she got from those pajamas still warms my heart when I think of that time. We got her all settled in, pillows positioned just right, enough blankets to keep her warm. My mom and my friend Nathan and I were all staying with her so she wasn't alone through the process. She asked us to play worship music, as she was settling into a scary reality and found comfort in the songs. The three of us were standing at the foot of the bed praising God for Sara. The peace that came over her face was majestic; I had known her for years and had never seen this level of calm and comfort on her face. She was radiant, with a gold-like glow to her skin. Where she seemed haggard and worn out now looked full and alive. Honestly, that image is still one of the most beautifully breathtaking images I have ever seen. It was so majestic that the three of us stood in awe with tears rolling down our cheeks, but they weren't sorrowful tears. If I had to describe them, they were full-circle tears. What I mean by that is they were tears celebrating a life lived.

I remember the peace in the room. I looked at my mom and whispered, "I think she has passed away. I think she is free from the torment that she had on earth." She had several things happen to her, as well as things that she had done that haunted her and were the cause of the guilt and shame. When we don't resolve the ghosts in our closet, they manifest in all shapes and forms. Sara was a beautiful young woman with bright brown eyes and olive skin. But like most people in the throws of addiction the drug use dimmed her physical beauty, when off of drugs she people would be totally captivated

80

by her physical beauty and engaging personality. When she used drugs and her life got unmanageable, that beauty went away and she looked haggard, old, and lifeless and riddled with guilt and shame. Kurt and I had seen this cycle with her on several occasions over multiple years. By the time she got admitted to the hospice in the patient part of the hospital, she looked depleted, deflated, and lifeless. To experience this transition of flat to full, with a glow of peace radiating off her, was breathtaking. She was beautiful inside and outside when she was off drugs, but in this moment shortly before she passed away, she was absolutely stunning, totally breathtaking.

We have reflected on that encounter for the last few years, and I never fully understood it until we began to examine the lake of fire. Today I believe her transition was an experience with the Creator of her life, purifying all of the distorted views and values that she had lived with, along with the guilt . I really believe that the lake of fire is a beautiful dance with the Trinity, allowing our eyes to fully focus on how wonderfully are we individually as well as all of humanity. Others focused is our God. The Creator of the entire cosmos intimately desires for us to be cleansed from all the areas where we lack clear vision and walk in the fullness that we were all created to live. That is what I believe happened to Sara that night. My mom, Nathan, and I got to participate in a beautiful unveiling of how wonderful Sara was beneath all of the distorted beliefs she had about her self. Shortly after that her eyes opened one last time, she told Nathan that she would see him again and they would swim in the Crystal River. Biblically, the Crystal River is the river that flows out of the tree of life in the throne room. The amazingly touching thing about that is Nathan was born with leg problems that resulted in his ankles being fused together. He has never been able to swim because his ankles won't perform the way they would need to kick properly. She glowed and radiated love and hope to him like I have never seen before. The nurse came in and said it was just a matter of time. Her heart was so compromised that her vitals were hard to read. Sara passed away surrounded by people who met her where she was, loved her unconditionally and never judged the situation that got her to this point. It was such a blessing to be able to be with her. Even in writing this now I have tears streaming down my face. I was blessed with getting to know Sara and loving her exactly where she was.

Oh, the freedom we can experience when we bask in the truth of who we have always been! The lake of fire is just like a wonderful day at the spa. Our distorted beliefs we have about ourselves are exfoliated off of us, allowing us to see ourselves as we truly are. No torture, no tormenting, no pain, no burning. Fully engulfed by God's love and light and ready to participate in the after-party worth writing home about!

What if, eventually everyone sees themselves the way God sees them, completely perfect?

Nine

SALVATION

Kurt's Experience

A few years ago, I was having coffee with a friend at a local coffee shop, when a group of five men sat down at the table behind us. I instantly recognized two of these men, one an associate pastor in the area and the other a leader in one of the area's local men's ministry. I assumed it was just a few friends getting together to enjoy a cup of Joe. But after a few moments I realized this was an event I now refer to as the "bait and switch." Three of the men had recently gone forward during an al- ter call at their church. An alter call is typically a plea from the pastor to get a show of hands of people who are finely ready to make a spiritual commitment to Jesus Christ. Then they are invited to come forward and repeat some form of repentance prayer and are instructed to meet with leaders for new believers at a future time. After the "new" believers come forward, the church usually hoots and hollers, spends some time high-fiving and patting each other and the pastor on the back for getting another one saved.

Sounds appealing, right? But, what I heard these two men tell the other three flabbergasted me. What came out of their mouths was downright disturbing and honestly one of the biggest reasons why many people outside of the church don't want anything to do with those inside it. "Even though you are not worthy to receive God's mercy or grace, you made the public proclamation to follow Jesus, and because of this you are now saved. But now that you are saved, you need to prove that when Jesus took the beating you deserved that his sacrifice for you was worth it." They then gave them a list of things they needed to do. Attend a new believer's group, tell others about their experience, invite others to go to church with them, and live without doing things the church sees as "sin."

Over the past few years, Katy and I have pondered much about what I heard that day, along with other forms of commitment rituals that churches endorse. From baptisms to confirmations, they all have similar patterns and they all stem from the same belief that we are not worthy, but thanks to Jesus we have a chance. They also always demand a person to quit committing dirty deeds to prove that their sacrifice was worth it.

The good news is that nothing can separate us from the love of God. (See Romans 8:31-39). Until recently, we didn't have a full understanding of this. Sure, we believed that nothing could separate us from God, Jesus, or the Spirit. But what does that really mean? If nothing can separate us from the love of God, then what are we saved from?

Most of the world's religions have some form of the "bait and switch." And they are quick to tell how right they are and how the church across the street is wrong. They claim you have to confess, repent, be baptized in water or even speak in tongues to be saved. These ideas have only fueled the fire that man is separate from God. Most Christian and Muslim denominations of today teach that we are separate from God. But we believe *everyone* is connected to the Creator of the world.

Many pastors teach that Jesus came to end the covenant system for the Jewish population, which was a sacrificial system of atonement. If Jesus came to end a covenant system and start a new one, then man must have needed to be saved from

84

something, which we do not believe was the case, and is still not the case today. We do *not* believe God was ever mad at man, and man never needed to be saved from him. No one was ever or ever will be out of His grace.

Jesus did save the Jewish population from the sacrificial system they had created to get atonement for breaking one or more of the laws they called God's laws, or any of the other 613 rules they came up with in an attempt to please a God who was already pleased with them.

For the rest of the world's population, the account of Jesus is a great reminder that nothing we could ever do would cause us to lose the favor or fall out of God's love. Jesus, who we see as the incarnate God, was convicted by the Jews, beaten and tortured at the demand of Jews, and hung on the cross and died at the hands of a group of people that could not see how such a loving, caring individual could be the Son of God. But Jesus rose from the darkness of Sheol, brought those that had died before him, with him, and ascended into Paradise with them. In Jesus we see the love and compassion of the Creator of *all* of mankind, who still loves and will always love even those who deny Him.

When we are able to see the rest of the world as God's chosen people, regardless of their beliefs then we begin to see the world the way God the Father has seen it all along!

Katy's Experience

I was sixteen years old when my mother volunteered me for a few hours a day after school to care for a neighbor of ours who was dying of cancer. This was a time in my life where my rebellion was at an all-time high. Not only because I was pushing back against anyone else's way of doing things, but also because I was in a place of learning what not to do in response to situations that cause character building and personal growth. I laugh now looking back on those times in my life. However, back then, I was stubborn, angry, and defiant to say the least.

Jan lived on the corner of a block tucked back in the woods overlooking the bay in Bigfork, Montana. Every day after school I would walk to her house. I had so many emotions at the time. She was a great lady, full of wisdom for being in her fifties. She was tall, thin and had stringy salt and pepper hair. She was fighting a battle with hip cancer. By the time I was involved she was bound to her chair in the living room. I would make her food, which felt very fulfilling. I was working at a restaurant at the time, and my whole life goal was to become a famous chef.

Jan was the first spiritual person I met. Mystical, thoughtful, guided by her beliefs. She had the presence of a Buddhist, coupled with a metaphysical side I didn't understand and, quite honestly, I stayed away from. Astrology signs filled her house as well as books about every religion lined her shelves. Looking back, I wish that I would have asked her what her foundational belief was. It was like walking into the eighth wonder of the world every day after school. There was comfort that I could be me one hundred percent of the time. She only had love and kindness, which radiated out of her. I could openly discuss with her the learning curve I was on in my life, and she never had anything but genuine acceptance and compassion. At that point in my life I was pretty guarded, so to have the ability to sit comfortably in my own skin and feel secure was a blessing for me.

The time that I spent with Jan got my mind thinking more about the big question in life: Is this experience on earth the only experience we have? I thought a lot about Jesus, not having any understanding, just wondering if he was real like I had heard. Or if he was just a folktale to give peace and allow some kind of meaning in the life we were currently living. I thought a lot about reincarnation, wondering is this really true I hope I am some majestic animal. The seven paths of enlightenment, which are mindfulness, investigation, energy, joy, relaxation, concentration, and equanimity, were all intriguing, I almost got overwhelmed with desire at being in that place of absolute peace. What I envisioned was bright, warm and vibrant. I came from no foundation spiritually, so thinking about these things stirred up more questions.

The day that Jan died I was present with my mom and another friend. It was very scary, because how can you ever prepare for what it's like to witness death? By this time, she was in a hospital bed that was set up in the living room of her house. Hospice was coming in to give her meds for comfort as well as the nursing and cleanliness side of home care. When I walked in the door that day, I knew it was going to be the last time I saw Jan. In the course of a day, she went from very ill looking to an unconscious skeleton of a person with thin pasty skin. My mind couldn't comprehend the decay of life I had witnessed during this time in my life. A deep bone-chilling rattle occasionally presented itself, and within a half an hour all aspects of life left her body. I stood by her side staring, overwhelmed by emotions that I am not sure I had felt before. This wasn't my first loss; my grandfather died when I was in sixth grade. However, this was my first loss since I had been deep in thought about what happens after this life.

We called the funeral home to come pick up the body. Jan had left a few instructions for what she wanted to happen after she passed. Her first request was to put her in her bright pink bathrobe. She wanted to be cremated wearing it. Looking back, it would have been easier if she would have been wearing that robe, because trying to put a corpse in a bathrobe while in shock of the situation I had just gone through was not easy. We had several laughs. Rolling her on her side, trying to get her lifeless arm in the sleeve and then the bathrobe underneath her body and her other arm in the sleeve, that still to this day may be the most awkward thing I have ever done.

At the time I left that house, I didn't have any fear about where Jan's spirit was. She was an incredibly loving, giving, vibrant person, full of what seemed like ancient wisdom. She had a peace about her situation that I couldn't wrap my head around. I remember looking at the clouds when I left her house and was driving. White as can be, fluffy like a marshmallow and vividly vast in the heavens above. I had total peace that she was in heaven with everyone who had passed in this world before. It wasn't a wish either. That security that I felt was deep in my soul, assurance and convinced.

After Kurt and I had our life changing, spiritually-charged encounter with God, I began to noticed the term would be used often in the "Christian community." When someone died, the first words out of most of these people's mouthed would be either, "Were they saved?" or "Do you know if they were a believer?" I always thought how that sounded arrogant. I will admit on my journey of trying to please God I found myself saying those same lifeless words. How is there any comfort for people who are grieving if the answer is no? This question never sat right in my heart, even though I read several bible translations that would elude to these words, I always felt conflicted about this. In my opinion, unworthiness and a separation allow us to cognitively try to justify that thinking. What I mean by that is, if our belief is that we are only made right by asking Jesus to be our savior, hoping that by doing so we will somehow make us present with the creator of all things, there can never be assurance and peace in our hearts.

Before any of these ideas are placed in our minds, a fundamental belief is everyone goes to heaven when they die. Ask kids who haven't been programmed with whatever theology they are exposed to. They will say Heaven. Always. The reason for that reality is "saved" and "unbeliever" are not a part of their original design.

This came abundantly clear to us at a friend's son's funeral. After the funeral, we were all gathered around to release balloons in Tom's honor. Upon letting the balloons go, Tom's niece, who was four or five years old at the time, yelled up to all the balloons as they got farther and farther away, "Tell Uncle Tom hi and that I love him." She never questioned that he was anywhere other than heaven.

The innocence that poured out of her pure heart that day hit us. Since then we have observed many small children playing together. Their parents might be concerned with the other kid's race, sexual identity, religion or lack of religion. But the children never are. They are just excited that they have friends to play and have adventures with. It is evident in those kids' face that they are truly one with each other and the one who created them.

Religion has made a list of things people need to do to be saved, when the reality is everyone gets to spend eternity in Paradise, dancing and playing with everyone who has ever lived and the One who created us in their image. God said, "Let Us create man in Our image"(-Genesis 1:26).

We have never been separated or lost from our Creator. Believing in ourself is believing in our Creator. Everyone is created in their image and likeliness, so when we are confident and trust ourselves, we are believing in the one who created us. Even if we are in a place where trusting ourself seems impossible and we are not experiencing confidence, we can take a deep breath. In that breath is the Creator's belief in us that we are worthy, we are loved and we are destined to live and enjoy life loved!

What if, God wouldn't keep any of His children from spending eternity with Him?

Ten

THE CREATOR

Our Experience

A few years back we got a call from a friend of ours whose nephew had been in the hospital for three months. Things looked very gloom, as he had recently been moved to a nursing home and they were looking for an adult group home that would be able to care for him the rest of his life . He was only in his mid to late twenties. Our friend's nephew had been a victim of a severe hate crime. The violators had beat him and carved a deep "swastika" into the inside of his upper thigh and he had been left to die. He was near death holding on and was rushed to the hospital by paramedics, who reported that he had died twice on the way and he was then in a coma for three months.

We were asked if we would be willing to come and pray for him. We said we would. Because of the crime and because all of the suspects were not in custody and the assault was still under investigation, law enforcement had to do a background check on us. We asked our friend Nathan if he wanted to go up with us at some point. He said he did, so they ran a check on him as well. The three of us were granted clearance to visit him during visiting hours.

The first day we went to see him just the two of us went. When we arrived at the hospital, we had to check in with guards who were stationed out side of his room before we went into his room. We had no idea what we were going to see or experience, but we believed we would see a miracle. He was sitting in a wheel chair. We found out from his Dad, sitting on his bed, that he had no use of his legs and had extreme difficulty talking. Paul's eyes were dark and filled with confusion, sadness, and fear.

We talked with Paul and his dad for a while. We found out that Paul was adopted, and the story moved us and still moves us. His dad was asked by a neighbor to give her a ride to the hospital. On the way to the hospital, he realized she was going to the hospital to have an abortion, so without any time to talk to his wife or think about it, he told the young lady "If you carry Paul to birth, I will take care of him the rest of his life." After listening to his story and finding out that Paul at the time he was assaulted had several young children, we laid our hands on him, anointed him with olive oil, and talked at length with God. Our prayer wasn't please, God, do this. It was Thanks, God, for what you have already done. Once done praying, we told Paul and his dad we would be back in a few days because we were headed out of town briefly for work.

When we got back into Kalispell, we called Nathan to see if he wanted to go with us to see Paul. He met us at the hospital, and the three of us checked in with the guards and went into Paul's room. Our friend John, who had called us initially was there, along with Paul's dad. John was standing, his dad was sitting on the edge of the bed, and Paul was sitting in his wheelchair. When we looked at Paul, his eyes were like light bulbs filled with peace, joy, and security. His speech had totally changed, and immediately he started showing us how he could move his legs towards his chest and kick them around. He told us that he had taken five steps since we had last seen him. Hearing him talk with clarity, seeing the spark in his eyes and hearing that he had taken some steps excited us. He told us that the doctors told him that once he could transfer himself from the wheelchair to the toilet on his own, they would consider releasing him from the hospital.

We found out that the doctors and nurses were in shock at the radical, supernatural change in Paul, as they believed his future was to be institutionalized. The five of us in the room praised God and thanked the Holy Spirit for continuing to heal Paul both mentally and physically. When our celebration had slowed down, Paul reached out and we helped him stand up. He stood up, did a little shuffle of a dance, and stood for a while on his own.

We visited Paul a few more times, and each time we saw miraculous improvements. He was released within a few weeks and spent the next few years living in another town, while the individuals faced the consequence of the hate crime they had committed. Last we heard he is doing well.

When we look back on this miracle, we see some amazing truths about who we are and who God really is. In part five of this section of the book, we wrote about the character traits of God the Father, the Spirit, and Jesus. How they all are only love. And in this love they are also *all* Holy, and not by the definition that we usually think of when we think of the word Holy, which relates to sacred or hallowed. But rather the Greek word *agios* means others focused. The fact that they are other focused is why Paul is able to walk, function, and talk today. But in that truth, God was not the author of the hate crime that happened to him. He was the creator of Paul's life from the beginning of time.

Sadly, God often gets a bad rap. Many experiences and events in life and the world have caused questions and doubt about who God really is. We have broken down and dissected the idea that God is the author of our life. If He is the author of life, then he must have traits of evil rather than only Love. If God authored all the sorrow, devastation, tragedy, terrorism, and natural disasters to happen or knew they were going to happen and didn't stop it, common sense would question how sick and demented God must be. Many times we have heard people say, "God doesn't give you more than you can handle." Our reply to that is, "Where does assurance and trust come from if you have buried your child to a suicide, lost a loved one to a horrific battle with cancer, or lost your family or friends in a horrible accident?

How could anyone who has experienced a horrific loss or a tragic situation find assurance from that statement?" We have heard others say, "God is giving you the opportunity to go through this to get closer to Him." Once again, we could never trust a God who did that or knew it was going to happen.. While thinking about how crazy that concept is, this story comes to mind. This story is not gender-specific. Imagine an abuse victim who has been brutally beaten, going to the hospital to get help. The doctor comes in and says to the nurses that they are stitching up the cut above the eye, stabilizing the broken arm, and securing the IV line. A person would not think, "Boy, I am so glad that this patient got to go through this, because now they have an opportunity to get closer to the abuser." Common sense says that is asinine and that doctor shouldn't practice medicine. Yet similar situations happen, and the leadership of church's say, "Boy, this is a great opportunity to get close to God, and by the way behave better so this doesn't happen again."

However, if God created our live, so we could live, experience, and grow through all of the experiences, situations, and encounters we have in our life, then God is off the hook for being seen as a tormenting jerk, and people have the opportunity to grow in relationship with a God who loves and cares about them through all the choices they make and situations that happen to them, with assurance that they are loved and secure people who are just experiencing life. God created all life, but He doesn't control everything. God does not cause murder, abuse, drug addiction, alcoholism, tornadoes, hurricanes, etc.

What if, God is the Creator of our lives, but *not* the author of any of the events of our lives?

93

Part Four

FOUR TRUTHS TO WALKING ON WATER

We have shared many personal experiences that caused us to look further into those eleven beliefs outlined in parts two and three that cause so much division and heartache in the world we live in. In Christianity, it is often taught that people need to be dunked in water to be saved. When John the Baptist saw Jesus approaching him he said, "This is the one who will lift the sin of the cosmos like an anchor from a sea floor for all of humanity to sail free." (-John 1:29 Mirror Bible)

He went on to tell his followers that he was commissioned to baptize with water but Jesus is the one who baptizes with the Spirit. (-John 1:33). Water is and always has been used to clean something that is dirty. In the Old Testament, Noah's ark is the symbolism that everything under the water is under God's judgement and the idea and teaching of dunking people under water at baptism is the same concept. The good news about this practice is that you come out of the judgement just as Noah floated above judgement. However, our belief is you were never dirty, and God has never judged you. (-John 5:22) Therefore, you are not dirty in God's eyes, and you don't need a bath for Him to love you and want to spend time with you. No dunk necessary! Just resting in the assurance that you are loved will keep you above the water. God doesn't judge; it's the world that is full of judgement. People judge each other, and individually we tend to be our own worst critic. The belief that we can live above judgement is foreign to those who who desire rewards for good behavior. If that's not hard enough, religion has painted a mythological judge and labeled him "God." Without the tools to guard our hearts from the lies of the "enemy," when we say enemy we are referring to distorted views, and beliefs we have about ourselves that make us feel "dirty" or unworthy at times, we can all fall victim to these forms of judgement. Just like we don't need to get made up to spend time with our best friends, we don't need to dress up to spend time with our Creator.

We stand on the truth that everyone in the world is God the Father's beloved child We are all brides, and the Spirit living in our heart is our best friend and she is also the perfect mother. Everyone has what it takes to walk above judgement. The good news lies in your identity. Knowing we are secure and OK gives us the ability to survive in the storms of life as well as create the lives each of us desires.

The next four truths we are diving into has given us the ability to move more into embracing love. Moving more into love has given us a way of seeing. We don't do it perfectly, however, since we embraced the first eleven topics together and allowed ourselves to walk into the freedom we found through those conversations. We now tend to build each other up in our weak moments. We call these topics four truths, because in the midst of them is spiritual truths or principles that apply to all walks of life. They are fundamental realities that, when applied, tend to allow healing to happen so that people can be freed from the burdens that weighs them down.

One

YOUR IDENTITY

Although we both had a time in our lives where we were very involved in the twelve-step community, and we still have friends involved in that culture. That chapter in our life has been closed for a few years now. We do not see ourselves as drug addicts or alcoholics. Through the process of discovering ourselves, we now know we used alcohol and drugs to cover up how we felt about ourselves. The *disease* that we both had around the foundational belief that we were OK exactly the way we were created, caused us both to stumble. We know that we are not the only ones who have experiences this.

Kurt's Experience

Earlier in the "your creator" part of the book, I wrote about how the day Katy was healed and how shame and guilt from being involved in the death of a childhood friend's dad had made me feel. Roughly five months later I went to a Narcotics Anonymous meeting to collect my annual coin at a birthday meeting, and then I went to share my gratitude for my new life. The protocol typically is "Hi my name is _____ and I am an addict." But that day I said, "Hi, my name is Kurt, and I am a father, husband, friend, brother and son." This was the first time I had broken ranks and didn't say I am an addict. During my entire share, I didn't say once that I was an addict. This was liberating, and even though it wasn't openly accepted as an appropriate way to introduce yourself in the meeting, it was a huge revelation in my life. I have never referred to my elf as an alcoholic or addict since. It wasn't long after that day that I quit attending any meetings. I attempted to go back a few years later after I was asked to share my testimony in both an AA and NA meeting. At that time, it became clear to me that I no longer could relate to that period in my life. I am forever grateful for those years of my life, because in it I met the love of my life, made some lifelong friends, and moved out of the darkness I was in and into what I call my gray years, I came out of the gray and into the light.

After that meeting, my life and how I viewed myself continued to shift. I realized that I was perfectly designed and loved by my creator. I am a child of God. I am husband. I am a dad. I am a son. I am a friend. I am a brother, and I was born to win!

One of the many gifts of life are relationships. We were not created to go at this "life" alone. So often our feelings about ourselves dictate the environment we associate ourselves with. Since we all desire relationships when we are at our lowest points, we tend to isolate or change our associations. An example of this is if we are feeling alone and not valued, we may think stopping off at a bar to be around people may be a good escape and ease the weight of the way we are handling stress. The first night we do this we may find such relief that we justify doing it again, thinking we are not hurting anyone or ourselves. Looking for resolve, we have all of a sudden found a culture of people who don't know anything about us and are more than willing to justify why we are feeling the way we are feeling. This causes a desire to stir up in ourselves that we are finally around "like minded' people. There is some truth in that. People secure in themselves may go through a phase and come to realize quickly that they are slipping. However, most of society tends to play to the level of life they associate with. This is not a criticism, it's a reality. So often in our searching for peace and relationship we end up in situations that temporarily allow us to feel OK, but usually they cause severe setbacks. This is why we feel understanding the way God sees us is such an important part to living our best life. Becoming comfortable and accepting of ourself, we will natural attract others who are comfortable and accepting of themselves, which in turn will create a culture that produces lasting results. When we guard ourselves with the truth that we were created to win, we can accomplish anything we desire and understand that we are foundation-ally good people. Naturally, we will respond out of that image. It doesn't take "deliverance" or an exorcism to change your life. It takes reconnecting with who you have always been. Sometimes this happens through relationships with other people.

Katy's Experience

Over the last few years I have begun to experience a shift in the way that I view myself. Yes, I still have moments where I don't see myself the way I should, and I get down on myself. I have learned this is a part of life, not an ailment. We all have moments of doubt and uncertainty. I think in those moments when the magnet is flipped and we reconnect with ourselves, we get to see more vividly, feel love more deeply, and have a more tangible life experience. Because we are finally in step with our purest self.

The summer of 2018 was a time of reconnecting. A relationship that shaped my formative years, gave me character, helped me discover my beginning quest for truth, loved me unconditionally and always told me I was more than I ever thought I could be, came back full circle after years of silence. In addition, we also went through some very uncomfortable situations. Together we found life, and we saw death first-hand in the home we had just moved out of and found ourselves blessed beyond measure, because God's perspective overwhelmed us both with joy.

As I woke up on my 36th birthday, I couldn't help but reflect on all the ways these little pieces of the puzzle are the Trinity's way of pulling us into the fullness of relationship that we have all been born out of and into.

Last summer I knocked on the door of Coaches house. Coach was my freshman and sophomore English teacher. As she turned the corner and we saw each other in person for the first time in nine years, because we currently lived hundreds of miles apart, it was as if there was absolutely no time gap since we had last seen each other. The familiarity, comfort, love and vulnerability hadn't changed even though we hadn't "worked" at maintaining our friendship. In fact, our relationship continued to grow so beautifully despite without any effort. It was simply because it has been there since our very first encounter. I believe today that this is how it is with the Trinity.

As I sift through the relationships in my life, the strongest, safest, and most secure are and have always been the ones that just "fit," no questions asked from the very first encounter. I am blessed that I have a handful of people who continue to mirror back what relationship with the Godhead looks like. By encouraging me and loving me always. Humanity is taught a system of steps, goals, concepts or ideas about "how to get to...", but God just says, Be. Be who I created you to be. Be the masterpiece that you are and be loved, accepted, complete, content, safe and secure and fulfilled knowing that you are in total union with the one who created you.

Love is the driving force of all things good. By beginning to experience that love, we begin to feed from the tree of life. When our hearts and minds are guarded in what has been true all along, lives begin to change. His life is manifested out of and through all His creation. Sometimes it's difficult for us to believe, but God is madly in love with each and every one of us. Even when it has been years since you felt or pursued a connection with Him. The truth is this connection has always been from the foundation of the world. His breath is your breath,

WHAT IF?

His life is your life and He is fully committed to lavish love on you, embrace you, and overwhelm you with the reality of who you are in Him.

We all are created out of love, in love, and for love. Nothing defines who we are better than love. Love is the bond that holds us together, changes our perspective, and sets us free to live and enjoy life. Love has no conditions. When we pour this love on people in our life, we show to the best of our ability the love of the Trinity.

A few weeks ago, Kurt posted on Facebook "I believe everyone is going to spend eternity in peace, love, and joy." The feedback was interesting. Many loved it, but there were those that got very upset. The ones who loved it seemed to feel a sense of peace in their heart, and those who didn't like it appeared to reflect a belief in a vengeful God. This difference in belief often causes division and arguments between family and friends.

When we are not sure if God loves all of mankind, fear and doubt reaches the inner most part of our heart. God's light begins to be overshadowed because of the anxiety this belief causes. However, when we come to the end of this road and begin to realize God is love and He has loved us and everyone else from the foundation of the world, His light expels the darkness caused by fear and doubt.

This simple post on Facebook ended up reminding us how very important it is to continue to share the love and acceptance of God with everyone we meet. This doesn't mean to preach at them about Jesus or even the things He did. This means to meet people in love, acceptance, and respect, right where they are. To do what Coach did for me when I needed to know love.

I have many relationships that reflect how awesome I am. These relationships have solidified my ability to be me. Authentic, transparent me. I am a strong believer that all people need these types of relationships. For me coach has always encouraged, loved and met me where I was at. She is such a great example of living in love.

You were created perfectly and authentically just the way you are. If there obstacles that are causing you to see yourself and behave in a way that you don't want to do, allow yourself to reconnect with yourself. Surround yourself with people who pull the best out of you. People who encourage and build you up. If you want to change the level of life you are performing, the best thing you can do is change your environment. Just like making a new friend, it's a process of getting to know yourself.

It's also a process of then walking into situations authentically. Taking the first step today and introducing yourself to the person you set aside long ago you will begin an amazing journey of joy, confidence and victory.

What if, Everyone is valued? What if, Everyone is loved and everyone is destined to live fully loved in union with their authentic self?

TRUTH NUMBER ONE:

YOU ARE PERFECT JUST THE WAY YOU ARE!

Two

OUR UNION

As we began to look at our relationship with God as tangible, we both desired applications in real life. So often God is described as some mystical untouchable being somewhere off in a mystical world, where he has a Wizard wand and depending on his mood or judgment of your behavior, he will wave his wand and blessings will pour out on you, or he will wave his wand and all sorts of bad things will happen as a point of correction in your life. We address how absurd that way of thinking is when we filter it through common sense. How can we ever be in union with something that seems light years away and sits outside of time?

Our Experience

The best book we have ever read that breaks down how in perfect union we are with the Creator of all mankind is the book Patmos by C. Baxter Kruger.

This past winter Katy was reading out loud from this book on a beautiful beach on the Big Island of Hawaii. A nice breeze was in the air, the surf was mild, and many were enjoying the warm clear water. Dozens of children were laughing and adults were taking in the sun. Beauty and love were all around us. In our many vacations to Hawaii, this was our first time at this beach. A recommendation from my uncle Mick and Aunt Laura, the beach is like a cove, with big massive lava rocks on each end and a stretch of white sand that runs maybe the length of six or so football fields. God's spectacular creation was everywhere we looked. The beach seemed like a meeting place for people from all the world and spiritual beliefs. Multiple languages were being spoken, and everyone had joy in their voices. It was obvious that people were enjoying life and reveling in the beauty of His Creation.

When Katy got to the chapter "Separation," everything got quite. Stillness filled the air and dozens of birds landed at or feet. Literally everyone and everything seemed to be intently listening to the words coming from her mouth. I stopped her in mid-sentence so she could see what had happened.

It dawned on us that what the whole world needs to know is that there is no separation from God. Whether you believe in Jesus, practice Buddhism, Hinduism, Native American traditions, are Agonistic or Muslim, there is no separation from you and whatever you believe created you. It doesn't matter your belief, where you come from, or any of that everyone and everything is in union with God. For us, we believe Jesus is the incarnate As we wrote in the section on "Your Creator," we are able to see the character and personality of God in Jesus and the Holy Spirit, and this allows us to have a healthy relationship with our Creator. We are able to openly talk to Him without fear of judgement. What Katy was reading that day resonated in everyone and everything on the beach that day, and their hearts all leapt with joy.

Patmos is a book about a man named Aiden, who has a conversation that changes his life. 'Aidan is a burned-out, suicidal theologian, who finds himself far from his native Mississippi, where he meets the Apostle John on the isle of Patmos. Beaten down by the modern world and desperate for

105

answers that his years of study have failed to satisfy, Aidan is confronted with astounding insight from the beloved disciple of Jesus. The two begin an extraordinary dialogue of truth and lies, revelation and deception, sorrow and joy. Through dreams and mind-bending discussions, the wise apostle exposes the lie of all lies about Jesus and our Father, leaving Aidan shaken to his core....but liberated.'

That day we saw what the too-good-to-be-true-news really does. Even the birds needed to hear it. The rest of our vacation we continued to read the book and finished it the night before we were headed back to Montana. When we got to the last chapter, we had to take turns reading because we both were sobbing with joy. This book changed our lives and shook us to the core... but it also liberated us and cleared up a major veil of confusion that had been blocking our vision of who God really is.

At our core, we believe that we are all connected, intertwined by the love of our creator. If we weren't, then empathy and compassion would never be a real emotion and narcissism would rule us all! In the identity part of this book we wrote about coming into relationship with ourselves. Union is coming into relationship with your Creator. No one is separated from the love of God, because all are in and of Him. The fear of not being included in God's family has tormented and tortured people long enough. Everyone is in union with God, and God will not divorce you. His love is the perfect unbreakable marriage that in sickness and in health will continue to grow. No one is cut off, left out, or abandoned. God is not a narcissist. For all eternity God is *love* and everyone is a part of that *love*!

What if, Living in union with humanity rather than looking for what separates us allows the tangible application of love? What if, we all began to look at people knowing that God loves them as much as God loves us?

We have said it before and will say it again. Nothing will ever separate you from God's Love. This is the Union of all unions, truly the union you can write home about, because nothing can ever break it.

TRUTH NUMBER TWO:

YOU ARE IN PERFECT UNION WITH THE CREATOR OF THE UNIVERSE!

Three

EXPANDING THE EYE OF
THE STORM

Throughout this book, we have shared situations in our life and experiences of growth or adversity-whether we are hit with health issues, financial issues, or relationships issues. Once again, we are drawn to an illustration that was depicted so well in the award-winning movie *Forest Gump*. For those of you who have not seen it, you may agree that Forest "thrived" through every adversity or hard time that he faced. In one scene Forest and Lt. Dan are on their fishing boat. A raging storm happens, Forest is fighting to keep the boat moving in the right direction. He gets thrown from side to side and exhausts himself in efforts to save the boat, as well as protect himself and Lt. Dan. All of a sudden, the focus changes from Forest working so hard to Lt. Dan sitting up on top of the poles of the boat getting whipped around. Gale force winds swing the boat back and forth, the sky is black. Lt. Dan is dangling in the wind, literally yelling and shaking a fist, "You call this a storm!"

Lt. Dan, who lost both of his legs in Vietnam, battles with serious rebellion, depression and addiction issues. But in this moment Lt. Dan, has been through enough and he rises up as high as he can and challenges the storm. Most of us have been through "storms" in our life that seem as if they are never going to end.

Just like Lt. Dan, we often get pushed to the edge of our sanity and yell and curse at the storm.

How do we all expand the eye of the storm in our lives, so that when these situations happen, we respond from a place of peace and reason instead of resorting back to old patterns of destruction? This is a huge question. Most addictions, destructive patterns, and emotional spirals come during or after huge storms in our lives. These behaviors and patterns form when we are trying to cope with whatever the unpleasant storm may be.

Our good friend and author of the health and fitness book *Bold Beyond Belief*, Taylor Reed said in a conversation we were having with him that, "Sex, death, and money are the three things that everyone will experience in their life, yet they are the three topics that no one wants to talk about openly." After he shared this statement, we pondered it and had a great discussion about it. Directly and indirectly, these three things are connected to most of the severe storms we all go through. We have shared many examples in this book of our experiences. These experiences have caused us to scratch our heads and examine the conflicts we have had in our hearts around beliefs we have been taught about how to handle or come to terms with the topics. In the Hell section of the book, the example, was Grandpa Jim and his fate of the afterlife. Many of the conversational topics we wrote about in Parts Two and Three started to happen during some extremely difficult times in our life, times when divine health and financial security seemed to allude us.

This next experience we are going to share was an incredible experience. Reflecting back on it now, we can see the imagery that God used to show us tangible evidence about why it is so important to guard our hearts with truth and love rather than suffocating ourselves with shame, fears, and lies.

109

WHAT IF?

Our Experience:

Four years ago, Kurt was asked to share his personal journey to a group of addicts. After he shared, we were approached by a young lady who was living in a woman's shelter. She was working hard to turn her life around and was taking the steps she needed in order to not return to the abusive rela- tionship that she had been in, one that had a long history of physical and emotional abuse. During our conversation with her, we could see the guilt and shame she had, but we also saw a glimmer of hope in her eyes. She told us she had a nine-month-old son. After a few minutes, we invited her and her son to come to our house for a home-cooked meal. She was overwhelmed by the invitation and agreed they would come. At this point we didn't know very much about her or how she had ended up living in a safe house.

When they arrived at our house, we sat down in our living room and started to talk while the dinner was in the oven. Immediately, we noticed how small her son seemed to be for being nine months old. To us, he looked like a newborn or at the most four months old. She proceeded to tell us that her son, who for the first several months had been in a terrible environment, was diagnosed with "failure to thrive" syndrome. This is when young children are not growing and developing the muscle and strength they should have at their age. Most cases are related to environmental issues and often have long-term effects. At this point he hadn't been able to lift his head. Until this encounter, we had only heard about this condition but had never seen anything like it. She explained that her son really didn't have a will to live and grow like normal infants. When she shared this with us, we asked if we could hold her son. She was more than willing, as she was overwhelmed by being a single parent and living in the situation she was in.

Kurt held him first. The baby was very weak, lethargic and didn't make eye contact. When our eyes met his, he had a blank stare as if he wasn't really present. Kurt laid him on his chest and began speaking words of life over him. I will never forget he told him, "You are so strong. You are God's masterpiece, perfectly loved and designed for great things." When Kurt spoke those words, he also stimulated the child's fingers, rubbed his back, and had a long conversation with the little guy. It was beautiful to watch. Over that next half hour as we were getting to know his mom, he was lying on Kurt's chest, when suddenly he scooted his elbows onto Kurt's chest and lifted his head up. He made direct eye contact with Kurt and the blank dull stare had been replaced with a sparkle in eyes. For the first time that evening it was obvious he was present and filled with joy. His mom was speechless; she couldn't believe what had just transpired.

After a few more minutes, Kurt passed him to me and I walked around telling him how much he was loved, how strong he was and that he was a world changer. I remember holding him and singing the song "Jesus Loves Me"while rubbing his chest. He began to make baby sounds and started to hum. The hum seemed to be his attempt to engage in the song I was singing. It was an amazing night.

During dinner Kurt and I took turns holding him and telling him how awesome he was while the other one ate. His mom was amazed at what she was witnessing. After a few more hours of them being at our home, it was time for them to leave. I handed the little guy back to his mom and she placed him in his carrier. She went to buckle the straps and, shocked, she said, "Oh my God! Wow!" We didn't know what was happening, so we asked her if everything was OK. She looked at us in total awe. Not only had he lifted his head and hummed a tune, but he had grown significantly in just a few hours of hearing how great and perfect he was and no longer fit into the car seat straps that had been used just a few hours before. We were all speechless, because in such a short period of us telling him who he really is, we had witnessed an amazing miracle by just enveloping him in love.

When they left, and we were overwhelmed and, honestly, somewhat stunned. Because of the excitement of what we had just witnessed, we felt moved to call our good friend's Joyce and Ed to share the experience. For the next few months we stayed in pretty close contact with the boy's mom, and she told us how amazed the medical community was for his breathtaking and miraculous turn around.

111

WHAT IF?

It had been a few years since we had thought about that night. When out of the blue the memory came to Kurt. After a short discussion about it, he said me, "This is such a good example of what it means to guard our hearts and expand the eye of the storm!" This boy was in a raging storm when we got introduced to him and he the doctors believed he had lost the desire to live. But when his heart was watered with his true identity, despite all the stuff he had went through that was no fault of his own, he shook off the blow he had received from life and rose his head, because in his darkness he heard the good news of who he is. In less than three hours he physically grew multiple inches and for the first time engaged in life-simply by hearing how wonderfully he was made and how much he was loved!

All of us have had storms and just like this young boy the way we make it through them is to surround ourselves with people who encourage, edify, and love us unconditionally. This is the too-good-to-be-true-news that changes people's life's. It saves people for anger, depression, addictions, and other things that are caused by not knowing how wonderfully made they are and how much they are deeply loved by the one who created them. It may not stop the storm, but it makes it more bearable.

The spiritual truth is that we believe about ourself we will become. And what we believe about ourselves comes from what we hear about ourselves. Often we have heard the great motivation of one's success is proving wrong, those who didn't believe in you which does work for many, whether it be temporary or everlasting. But hearing how perfectly you are designed and how wonderfully made you are is how you get back up when you get knocked down.

One of the greatest examples of self-talk was the late and great boxer Muhammad Ali, who talked often and freely about how great he was and how he was the greatest of all time. He talked so much that his belief in himself continued to grow and grow.

Even after devastating defeats, he got back up, told himself and the world that he was still the greatest, and would often create a rhyme about how and when he was going to knock out the guy who had just whooped him. And guess what? He would end up doing what he promised!

In the middle of storms like tornadoes and hurricanes, there is a calming center that is total peace and serenity called the eye of the storm. We can have a raging storm going on in our life, from health issues, financial stress, to struggling relationships. But, when we know and are being reminded of how much we are loved and the great value we have, the peaceful center of the storm expands, and the storm seems to disappear.

What if, we all knew that God loved us unconditionally? What if, we all knew that we were designed perfectly?

TRUTH NUMBER THREE:

REMINDING OUR HEARTS WITH ASSURANCE THAT WE ARE OK, GIVES US THE CAPACITY TO MAKE IT THROUGH ANY STORM WE FACE IN LIFE !

Four

LIVING IN EDEN

The Hebrew word for *Eden*, used in the story of Adam and Eve, means *pleasure*. Adam and Eve were in the Garden of Pleasure. The English word *pleasure* means satisfied and fulfilled. When we know our identity and the perfect union we are in, the eye of life's storms become the Garden of Pleasure. We begin to experience the life we are *all* destined to live.

Our Experience:

During the time Katy was sick, we accumulated significant medical debt that, due to bad decisions, increased significantly. We worked hard, prayed hard, and bought into the idea we needed to tithe. The only reason we didn't drown is because we kept swimming and didn't throw in the towel. During this time in our life, we read a lot of self-help, motivational books. We attended weekend seminars about how to become successful network marketers, listened to hundreds of hours of motivational testimonies of people who started off broke and achieved financial success. All these things, and our good friends renting one of their houses to us at a pro-rated price, kept us afloat. We were building a networking business, working for merchandising companies, and painting a few houses here and there. Our bank accounts were constantly in the red, our paychecks were being garnished by bill collectors.

When the revelation that we are always going to be provided for began to sink in, our life began to change. By this time, we had seen dozens of miraculous physical healings, but very few supernatural financial turn arounds. As we mentioned earlier, when we began to come out of the darkness and into the light. We didn't know it, because we hadn't been involved in Christianity before this time, we were connected to the "Word of Faith Movement."

The Word of Faith Movement's major emphases are healing the sick, speaking in tongues, and being financially prosperous. They teach "physical, emotional, financial, relational and spiritual healing for those who successfully operate in God's laws. The movement urges believers, to speak what they desire, in agreement with the promises and provisions of the Bible, as an affirmation of God's plans and purposes." What they mean is if you are broke, broken, or sick, you are failing to live up to the standard God has for you, which determines the level of success you have.

What we began to believe was that in order for us to stay healthy, we needed to pray and lay hands on everyone we could that was sick. We also felt we needed to spend a majority of our spare time in prayer. We saw our financial struggles continue and we believed the result was from not tithing enough. We believed that God was only going to give us wealth when He believed we would be good stewards of His money.

Over the years the teachers, theologians, and pastors have changed. We spiritual grown past many the ones we once listened to on a regular basis. Which allowed us to understand the movement we were initially exposed to in 2011, and why at times we felt deep condemnation that we weren't doing enough. When we started to see that God loved and really liked us, minor shifts began to happen. The love we felt from our Maker started to grow in our hearts, In February of 2016, while on a weekend excursion to Las Vegas with friends, and during a time when the storm in our life was blowing hard, Katy's dad had been diagnosed with cancer. The merchandising company we were working for had grown significantly, and they didn't have the structure set in place to handle the growth. Our plan was to use the weekend to decompress and look at what changes we needed to make in our life.

We made the decision to quit our jobs and the network marketing company we had been involved with for seven years. Our plan was to start painting more houses so Katy could help care for her dad. The next few months were very interesting, Katy's dad passed away, and we decided to partner up with another painting contractor. Our son, Zac, got married during this time. Everything in our life got swept up in the storm, and we seemed to be going in all directions. But in the chaos of a funeral and dealing with loss, a new partnership, and a wedding, we were exposed to a different take on "end time and second coming" teachings from what commonly taught in the church.

We quickly moved out of eschatology, which is the study of end times and into how we see God and how he really sees us. This shift from what we need to do to what He thinks about us gave us the freedom to begin to live and enjoy life. We started to watch TV and movies again and listen to music that isn't endorsed by the Christian community. In this freedom, our vision of God grew, we began seeing more and more that He is only a lover and this really changed, how we thought He viewed us. We started to save more money than we were even making-our money was now multiplying. We started putting money in an envelope in our top dresser drawer. We would put a hundred dollars in the envelope and then when we went to put another few hundred dollars in the envelope, the hundred we had put in before was now several hundred. This continued to happen each time we put money in the envelope. Five months later we had accumulated enough money to take a thirty-five-day vacation that started with a few days in Colorado Springs, twenty eight days in Florida to see the sights and family, and ended in Las Vegas.

The following year and half we stayed in our painting partnership. We ran the jobs and he delivered the supplies to the job sites and did the majority of the bidding. On paper we were starting to do better; we went on a few vacations, as our belief in who we truly were was growing. Then in February of 2018, while in Hawaii on vacation, we made the decision to end the partnership and take the jump off the diving board and operate our own company again. Although we had done this in the past, this time we both knew in our hearts that it was different now because we saw ourselves differently.

To others this seemed like a gamble. We had one job lined up that was less than a week's worth of work for the two of us, with zero leads on other work. When we got back from Hawaii, we let a few people know what we were doing, and our phone began to ring. We started to line up work. We drove through neighborhoods and said to each other, "That house needs a new paint job, looks pretty easy. It would sure be nice to paint that one," and within a few days the owner of the house who we didn't know, would get ahold of us, saying they would like us to paint their house. This hap- pened multiple times, and in most cases the people didn't even get other bids.

Quickly our schedule was full, and we brought in a few people to work with us. The massive debt seemed to get paid off supernaturally. Things haven't slowed down and our business continues to grow. Our financial testimony isn't to brag, cut it is meant to share that once the truth of our identity had been watered and fertilized, we began to live as if, not begging or pleading and hoping things would work out, just living and acting as if they were already taken care of. Because we realize that God's love has no condition our mindset has shifted from lack to abundance and this has changed everything in our lives.

Another spiritual truth is our mouth speaks what our heart believes. When the seeds of wrong belief are plucked out of our hearts, the things that we had dreamt about become, possible and we begin to create the life we desire to live.

We believe everyone was created in God's likeliness and image, and God is a creator. Therefore, we are all capable and designed to create. We can all meditate on what we want our life to become; knowing we are worthy of it helps our dream become our reality.

WHAT IF?

There are many self-help books and seminars about how to have successful relationships, divine health, or to have a prospering business. Many of them have sound principles and can help you shift your thinking from seeing yourself as a failure to living as a success.

What if, you have been created to create the life you desire?

All the topics we have written about are meant to encourage you to create a dialogue with yourself and with others geared toward seeing yourself and others the way God sees you. In most religions and philosophies, a few simple principles are true when it comes to creating and living the life you desire in your heart. Anyone without a goal or goals will eventually rot from the inside out and those who talk about or write about their goals and dreams will eventually achieve them. The desires of our hearts were never meant to lay dormant or be hidden deep inside us. They were given to us so we can embrace the inward relationship with our authentic selves. This path of unveiling the desires we have is a incredible journey of losing the shame and guilt that have wrongfully been placed on us and clearing up the vision that we were born to live a life of abundance.

TRUTH NUMBER FOUR

YOU HAVE BEEN CREATED TO CREATE AND LIVE THE LIFE YOU DESIRE!

Part Five

THE CONTINUATION

WHAT IF?

We have been able to see and experience some amazing supernatural events over the last decade. In many of the testimonies, we have shared what happens when the good news of our identity comes out of us and others. The good news is the transforming information that changes lives and heals the broken hearted.

Sadly, we have seen multiple cases where people got better and then, over a period of time, ended up with the same ailments. These cases baffled us for many years. We realize that in most of those cases the individual who was healed went back to the same routine, plugged back into the same religious groups they had been involved in and didn't water themselves or have others watering them with truth about who they are and who God is. From our experience, watering and being watered is vital to continuing to live and enjoy life to the fullest.

We also know that sometimes wrong beliefs about God and ourselves have been planted and re-planted many times in our lives. Because of some of those deep seated events and beliefs, it makes sense to seek people who have been trained in those areas to help us clean out the closet.

The experiences and testimonies we've described were events we have had on this journey. Many of these events helped us to get to where we are now, by moving to examine certain topics that caused us and others to stumble. They also led us to take a hard look at what we consider four major truths that have helped us live and enjoy life.

After discussing and dissecting the goat, the ten elephants, and the four truths, we were able take a deep breath and confidently and comfortably live in our skin. For us, this conversation started in our hearts with the Creator of the universe, early in our childhood and progressed rapidly after certain events happened in our lives. When we discussed openly the things that never resonated in our hearts, we heard and found the love of God. This Love showed us the truth that has set us free.

Everyone has stuff. We all have experiences we go through that build layers of hurt that act like blinders over our hearts. Our belief is by being vulnerable and talking about the compartments of our hearts that are heavy or hurting, healing will happen. Whatever the struggle may be-addiction, pornography, adultery, narcissism, self-esteem issues, financial struggles, parenting issues, and other relationships. The same rule applies. Know you are loved!

Whatever may be going on in your life right now, we encourage you to take a deep breath. Fully breathe in and slowly exhale. In the midst of this moment of calm, know that the Creator of your life gave you that breath and in that breath is life. As long as we are breathing, we have the chance of experiencing a different outcome, one that leads us away from pain toward *happiness*. Also say to yourself, "I am OK. I am loved. Everything always works out for me!" Say that more than once. We know it sounds simple, but if you string a series of breaths and affirmations together, over time your reaction will be to breathe and remind yourself how awesome you are. Over time you will begin to change your vision and the way that you see yourself. Also, your ability to handle situations will radically turn around.

By now this whole discussion boils down to two incredible truths: First, You are loved beyond measure and second, designed perfectly. The movie *Rocketman,* is a radical depiction of what the unraveling process looked like for Sir Elton John. The movie starts out with Elton, leaving right before he is supposed to perform in Madison Square Garden and admitting himself into treatment. He ends up walking into his first group, emotionally broken and disconnected from himself, wearing the flamboyant costume and makeup he had put on to perform.

After every event he shared in the meeting, certain parts of the costume would be removed. He went from being fully dressed in a costume to being nude, and then by the end wearing everyday clothes. The symbolism of the way the story is told was completely relatable to us. Maybe because our initial journey together began much like the opening scene in the movie-the stripping of one's persona being put out to the world in order to be comfortable with one's self. The hurt and tragedies he had experienced in his childhood influenced most of his life and caused him to make many decisions to attempt to change how he viewed himself. His story isn't unique, and the moment he became comfortable with who he is was extremely beautiful.

Many of us have attempted to be someone we are not in a group setting; we put on a false front and pretend to be something we are not. But just like Sir Elton John, we ended up tired, feeling broken, and eventually took off the false front and got comfortable in our own skin. Everyone can take off the costume they have on and live from their authentic design in love.

Kurt's Experience

The summer before my Grandpa Jim passed away, my mom took her parents with us to California on a three-week vacation. It is one of the best memories I have of Grandpa Jim and Grandma Audrey. We loaded up in our family's truck camper and made the journey. Along the way we stopped at a few relatives' homes, went to several baseball games, played lots of cards, hung out on beaches, swam in pools in some hotels, and went to DisneyLand.

122

Grandpa Jim had already had a few heart attacks at this point, but he didn't allow that to slow him down. He still played catch with my brothers and me and told great stories and jokes. One of the relatives we stopped at was his brother Harry. This was the first time I had ever heard about Harry, who was his youngest brother and lived in the Bay Area. I found out that they hadn't talked in a few decades because Harry, who was a successful accountant, had left his wife because he was gay and this caused my grandpa to have a major issue with him. When we stopped at Harry's house, we all talked for a while and then my grandpa and Harry went into the pool area of his house by themselves. My grandma and mom seemed very nervous, and this is when I heard them talking about Harry being gay. They were both proud of my grandpa for wanting to go see Harry and make amends with him and to finally accept him for who he was.

When they came out of the pool area, it was obvious they had both been crying, but they seemed to have a great bond. I never heard exactly what was said, but after that day, Harry was a part of our lives until he passed away years later. I often think about that day and the courage my grandpa had to admit he was wrong. For my own life I can see this as a great example to love people just the way they were made. Love always wins!

Another one of our favorite scenes in *Forest Gump* is when Lt. Dan is sitting on the dock as Forest passes by him in his boat. The moment Forest sees Lt. Dan, he jumps off his boat and swims to the dock to embrace him. Forest just jumped in and never thought about his boat, which had no one else on it. He never thought about the depth of the water he was jumping into, nor did he think about the cur- rent he may encounter. He simply jumped in and rushed to embrace his old friend, full of love and excitement. The way Forest embraced Lt. Dan is very much a picture of how we can embrace our inner voice and beliefs that have been covered and silenced by life's situations.

123

WHAT IF?

Katy's experience

Years ago, I was a part of a woman's spiritual retreat. During one part of the weekend, the woman had a time where they are able to go to a prayer station and pray. I had been asked to lead one of prayer stations. A friend and I were partnered up at the station and it was a powerful experience. One of the ladies that came forward for prayer was really struggling. I could see that there was deep hurt and sadness by the way she carried herself. She shared her heart with us that she could not stop having affairs. She said she had tried everything she could think of to change this behavior. She described the frustration and she got very vulnerable with the situation that was destroying her marriage, her inward peace and her belief that she could change. The courage this woman had to open up and share her heart was so beautiful. Sometimes I think the most beautiful moments of our lives are the most painful. Upon listening to this woman, I began to see how weighted down we can get in our searching for community and truth..

Like most of us, when we let our guards down our minds get flooded with horrific thoughts about how stupid we can be for sharing or exposing ourselves. While she was so broken, I remember saying to her "What if ? What if instead of trying to quit the affairs, you just start to see yourself without the desire to have the affairs?" I remember telling her to try this even on the way to having the affair, even in the act itself. I suggested to her that if she could see herself whole and complete it will build up the resistance against the actions she is taking to try to find completion. It's a shocking statement, I know. I really feel that people don't need to be told what they are doing is wrong; condemnation is never the catalyst for lasting change. Condemnation can temporarily make someone behave differently, just like will power. However, the day always comes that the choice to behave that way again is stronger than the belief we can overcome it. Hence the vicious cycle begins again.

Everyone has obstacles in their pathways to live a loved life. This message isn't just for people having affairs. It's for everyone. Addictions, unworthiness, shame, guilt. The unveiling begins when we can become vulnerable and allow the pressure gauge to be released.

Having assurance is the key to overcoming adversity. The biggest deception we have as humans is thinking we are the only ones experiencing or going through the experience we are in at the time. When we can be real with ourselves, we see most people have the same problems.

Embracing the unknown and coming to your own conclusion is where freedom happens and living free really begins. We have both talked in depth with each other about certain theologies only lasting until a life event causes people to question or challenge that view. We know we are not unique, and it has been interesting as we have had conversations with others about these topics that most of the time we hear, "Wow! I have always had those questions. Just never had someone I could talk with them about." We love having these conversations. We don't claim to have all the answers. We just know that talking about our questions and finding answers has expanded our hearts to look at different concepts and create our own conclusions for where we are today. That being said, we also know that the unveiling continues as circumstances present themselves in our lives.

Having the freedom to be allows beautiful experiences to happen. Being open allows us the ability to see the best in people and encourage them on their journey. Life isn't a cookie-cutter, one-size-fits-all experience. Rather it's multi-dimensional, full of color, with different views. In regard to this, Martin Luther King Jr, said it best in his "I have a Dream" speech. Coupled with observing small children interact, the pureness and innocence of their hearts shine through until they have outside influences speak into them. Naturally, they operate from a place of love and vulnerability. We are so excited that tomorrow we will wake up and know that our experiences will shape our conclusions. The longest journey man will ever take is from the heart to the head. We have everything good in our hearts; sometimes we just need to flush out the nonsense that pollutes our heads.

We hope that the juices of thought are flowing and propelled by *What if ?* Asking *What if ?* allows the walls we put up to come down and the journey from black and white to expand into a full-spectrum color experience. Thank you for being a part of our discussion.

Now it is your turn! The questions that weigh you down are the ones worth discussing! The discussion deflates the elephants and changes the way we view the goat, pushing the old ideas and ways we view ourselves out of chambers of the hearts, so you can finally take a deep breath and enjoy the peace of the moment you are currently in.

You are blessed! You are loved! And you are free to live life in peace and joy!

Be blessed as you continue your journey into Love.

In Love, Kurt & Katy

Made in the USA
San Bernardino, CA
08 May 2020